CHOOSE YOUR OWN INQUIRY!

**Randy Ai, Mihir Bhatt, Stephanie Chevrier,
Robert Ciccarelli, Rosheen Grady,
Vandana Kumari, Kayi Li, Natasha Nazarali,
Hanieh Rahimi, Jillian Roberts,
Jonathan Sachs, Andrew Schepmyer,
Michael Wang, and Henry Wong**

D1333553

University Press of America,® Inc.
Lanham · Boulder · New York · Toronto · Plymouth, UK

Copyright © 2008 by
University Press of America,® Inc.
4501 Forbes Boulevard
Suite 200
Lanham, Maryland 20706
UPA Acquisitions Department (301) 459-3366

Estover Road
Plymouth PL6 7PY
United Kingdom

Library of Congress Control Number: 2008925816
ISBN-13: 978-0-7618-4092-3 (paperback : alk. paper)
ISBN-10: 0-7618-4092-3 (paperback : alk. paper)
eISBN-13: 978-0-7618-4214-9
eISBN-10: 0-7618-4214-4

TABLE OF CONTENTS

Preface

We wish to enlighten scholars, educators, parents and students alike that there exists an alternative method of teaching that is challenging and may be more effective in some cases than the traditional lecture-based pedagogy to which we are all accustomed. Through gripping narratives reinforced by a wealth of qualitative research, this book will allow readers to question the effectiveness of the dominant style of instruction that currently pervades Canadian universities and secondary schools. Once readers enter and understand the world of Inquiry, they may not view conventional education the same way again. This sense of discovery and revelation is exactly what we wish to achieve. Prepare for a truly unique journey and look through our eyes at a community of learners you may not have thought possible.

This book evolved with the inspiration from student experiences in the Bachelors of Health Sciences Program at McMaster University and the need to share our story with the international academic community in a comprehensive context. Inquiry is a core element of this program. It is a collective process shared by all undergraduates which demands intellectual innovation and development of the inquisitive mind. BHSc. students pursue a core Inquiry class each year that helps to develop and put into practice the essential learning skills. Other BHSc. classes provide an environment which promotes application of these skills to specialized subject matter varying from Cellular Biology to Creative Writing. The goal of such an encompassing arrangement is to foster the attitude of collaboration among students and allow them to direct their own learning and growth.

The Inquiry method, developed at McMaster University, expands conventional education parameters by shifting power from teachers to students and promotes the creation of a collaborative community of learners. In this environment, students are provided with opportunities by facilitators to explore, question, and construct knowledge while developing skills such as critical thinking, communication, time-management, group learning, and self-evaluation. In developing these learning skills, process is centralized to highlight the principle of lifelong learning.

We use a narrative style to present the students' frustrations, rewards and lessons, as we feel it is the most encompassing approach to reflect the essence of Inquiry. This style captures the richness of information from our student sources and the broad continuum of meanings associated with Inquiry. In understanding the effectiveness and limitations of this process in a book format, the reader will come to grasp the same learning tools used by our students.

The unique writing style of the book was borne when a wonderful childhood experience was recalled from *Choose Your Own Adventure* novels. In many facets, the fundamental elements of learning draws back to its persistent, inquisitive motivation that is inherent in our younger years. The readers of our book will be provided with flexibility that allows for self-directed exploration throughout the narrative. Each section of the book offers several routes that a reader can choose for continuing his or her journey through Inquiry depending on his or her curiosity, feelings, and interests.

We owe much gratitude for the numerous students and faculty members whose contributions were essential in producing this book. An unprecedented initiative, this narrative reflects an enormous collaborative adventure. Our goal is to enable readers to experience the thematic aspects of Inquiry, from frustrations and anxieties in learning curves to the triumphs of epiphanies and self-discovery.

-    The Inquiry Team

McMaster University
Hamilton, Ontario, Canada

June 2006

Acknowledgments

We would like to thank a number of individuals for their support and encouragement throughout our Inquiry adventure.

Dr. Sheila Barrett, *for her patience and guidance*
Dr. Patangi Rangachari, *for his insights into Inquiry*
Dr. Delsworth Harnish, *for his support and encouragement*
Dr. Chris Knapper, *for his insights into the writing process*

We would also like to thank the following groups of people for their support. Without their cooperation and enthusiasm, this project would not have been possible.

The BHSc students, *for supporting the project with their participation and encouragement*

The BHSc office staff, *for providing us with equipment, resources, and support*

The Clinical Learning Centre staff, *for providing us with a standardized location to conduct our research*

Benchmarking–Part I

Nervousness, curiosity and excitement fill the atmosphere of an otherwise dull classroom. Students have heard the term Inquiry as being a key aspect of the Bachelor of Health Sciences (Honours) Program (BHSc), but anxiously await a definition. They soon find out that the definition of Inquiry will not be handed to them on a silver platter: not now, not ever. Inquiry is theirs to discover, theirs to experience.

Learning and development in Inquiry is gauged through progress. All first year BHSc students complete an activity called benchmarking at the beginning and end of their Inquiry journey. This activity is completed in a group and requires students to read an abstract from a scholarly journal, form questions based on the abstract, refine their questions, and seek answers to those questions. Benchmarking allows students to develop a sense of where their research, critical thinking, communication, and group work skills are before the Inquiry experience. The same group of students repeats the exercise at the end of the course as evidence of learning and progress.

This is your own benchmarking experience, a chance to mark the beginning of your journey towards understanding Inquiry.

Benchmarking Exercise

Please take a moment to answer the following questions:
1.   What makes an educated person?

2.   What is learning?

3.   How do you learn?

4.   If you had to ask one scholarly question, what would it be?

5.   How would you find an answer(s) to the question you asked above?

   After working your way through this manuscript, you will have the chance to revisit these questions and gauge your learning.

Topic 1: Education, University and Inquiry

Thinking

Box 1.1
 	
 Outside the Box
 	
 Teachers often encourage students to think beyond familiar boundaries. However, the classroom structure can be counterproductive to the goal of creative learning. Much of this paradox has to do with the loss of control and increased feeling of vulnerability when choosing to wander from beaten paths. It is an unsettling feeling to put oneself out into the open and say something that others may find ridiculous. Sometimes though, one's decision to take those kinds of risks is the beginning of an inspiring vision.
 	
     Our Inquiry Team struggled for weeks to come up with a format to organize our book. The first reaction for most of us was to jump into examining education literature. We envisioned a conventional product, a book made of linear chapters, and each focused on an Inquiry theme. Our content would be based on literature reviews and our own quantitative research findings. We were going with what we felt was most familiar and comfortable to us. It certainly sounded like the "right" idea.
 	
     Intuitively, however, we felt something was missing. How would we truly capture the intimacy, the vitality, and the spectrum of emotions that come through the Inquiry experience? Then one day, one courageous group member proposed a radical idea. Fortunately, the rest of the Inquiry Team withheld judgement and listened. "Do you remember the *Choose Your Own Adventure* books that we read when we were kids? Why don't we do something like that?"
 	
     In case you are unfamiliar with the series, the *Choose Your Own Adventure* books are designed to put the reader right into the narrative. Throughout these books, the reader, playing the role of a main character, is presented with choices

that influence the direction in which the story unfolds. Since each reader may choose a different path, numerous endings are possible. Our Inquiry Team wished to adopt a similar format to engage our readers in an individualized, self-directed journey. We continued discussing and building upon each other's ideas as one interpretation led to another. By the end of that meeting, we had developed a new and exciting direction for our book.

The rules and tools that have been drilled into our minds by formal education are useful. However, the strength of intuition and imagination should never be underestimated. Many ways exist to solve a problem. Be daring!

What is Learning?

From cradles and sandboxes to classrooms and boardrooms, everyone engages in learning from the day they are born until the moment they die. Despite its inarguable impact upon our lives, there remains much to be understood about this remarkable phenomenon. What types of learning have you engaged in over the past month? Take a few minutes to reflect and jot down your ideas. Consider this to be a part of your exploration of Inquiry.

The values of the society in which people live influence how they feel about learning. The meaning and perception of learning differ between cultures. Our exposure to a traditional pedagogical curriculum can make it hard to think of learning without conjuring up images of classrooms, perhaps a teacher giving lectures, distributing homework, and administering tests.[23] Our values influence the motivations for higher education. For example, most people go to school today so that they may be well prepared to enter the workforce. This approach and motivation for learning is quite different from that experienced by others throughout history. A few historical examples are given in Box 1.2. Take a look!

Indeed, education has been viewed in many different ways throughout history. How do you think these views compare to our current understanding of learning?

---

[23] How else can it be, you ask? When you think of learning, you do not necessarily have to envision such typical scenes. Look through our eyes; turn to page 23!

Box 1.2

In Ancient Greece, the Socratic method of teaching emphasized discussion between teacher and student, as they explored philosophical questions. Through the interchange of logical arguments, a cycle of questions, answers, and new questions, students were trained to reason effectively and to think critically, rather than simply receiving information passively (Cicchino, 2001).

In 18th century Europe, education's purpose was to eliminate the unfavorable traits with which humans were born. Learning was geared towards the development of desirable traits, almost like a spiritual remedial. Learning through books was not employed in an attempt to gain knowledge, but to foster the development of children into mature, polite, and moral adults (Arizpe & Styles, 2004). The teacher's role was to facilitate the transformation of a morally flawed student into a more "ideal" individual (Vanderstraeten, 2001).

In traditional Native American education, learning was about sharing personal feelings and experiences, serving others, and connecting with nature. Education reflected the value of community and the idea that life integrates mental, physical, spiritual, and emotional elements (Simonelli, 1996).

Tribes in India in early 19th century focused on intellectual and moral development through experience-based education. Children gathered in informal learning houses in the evening to share stories, riddles, and songs (Bara, 2005).

During the late 19th century, American philosopher and psychologist John Dewey designed a classroom design where learning was encouraged through group-based projects, emphasizing skill and knowledge application. For example, rather than learning about fractions by doing problems out of math textbooks, students would be guided to acquire this knowledge in the real-life context of construction, where understanding fractions is necessary for making correct measurements.

Dewey believed that a child's natural qualities, curiosity, the ability to question, and the natural desire to grow and build, should drive learning. Ultimately, Dewey felt that learning should promote a democratic society. In the classroom, this vision was reflected as children worked and learned together, while taking on roles which simulated societal vocations (Dewey, 1897; Dewey, 1916).

Education As We Know It

Education "as we know it" is heavily influenced by a teacher-centred model, which we will henceforth refer to as traditional pedagogy. (The term "pedagogy" is derived from the Greek word paidagogos, which refers to the slave whose role was to chaperone children to school). Under this paradigm, students are considered to be blank slates onto which teachers transfer information. Such a structure of education introduces several important consequences that alter the way learning occurs in the classroom (Ozuah, 2005):

(a) Learning is based on knowledge of specific, predefined topic areas.
(b) Students are seen as passive receivers of information who do not possess the capability of directing their individual learning.
(c) The teacher rarely considers the baseline knowledge, skills, goals, and experiences of the student.
(d) Each class runs independent of others and presents a discrete, formulaic package of information that lacks a concern for students' personal lives.

These ideas have profound effects on education. First, let us examine how communication occurs in the classroom. Under the model of traditional pedagogy, there is unidirectional transfer of information from teachers to students. The teacher is the focal point of communication since information cannot be delivered without his or her presence. In the context of universities, information is transferred in lectures, in which the teacher provides answers to eager students whose main responsibility and focus is to take up information, like sponges absorbing water (Vanderstraeten, 2001). Student learning in the teacher-centred classroom is based heavily on content, and information is stored in students' minds until it is required for further use in exams or other forms of evaluation.

Traditional pedagogy also shapes learning objectives. The typical course of education can be described as "programmed learning," whereby the teacher assigns specific learning goals that drive student learning (Postman & Weimgartner, 1969). Despite the course design having little consideration for students' interests or personal motivations, students are discouraged from altering it. In fact, the teacher keeps students in check through the distribution of rewards and punishments. Reflect upon your own experiences and you may notice that this method has influenced your learning. Think back to the stickers you received each time you finished reading a book and recall the scolding that followed when you did not complete the task. Even in art, a subject that emphasizes individuality and creativity, students are often taught to mimic the teacher's models and are awarded a grade based on the level of imitation. For the majority of students, this approach to education has persisted in higher education institutions, except stickers and scolding are replaced by grades and scholarships.

Is there a problem with this approach to learning? First, while didacticism may facilitate the role of the teacher, it is often ineffective for student learning (Banning, 2005). Lecturing can be useful when trying to introduce key principles behind a course, but it doesn't provide opportunities for student participation or rumination. Furthermore, the structure of a teacher-centred classroom simply isn't realistic. Guidelines do not exist in real-life, and any interaction between two or more people can take many unforeseen twists and turns. Although a teacher's role as the creator of objectives works in a traditional classroom, it is inapplicable to the real world where interactions between people do not follow such unidirectional dynamics (Vanderstraeten, 2001). Additionally, since the teacher determines what is learned in a traditional classroom, students find it difficult to see its inherent value and lose internal motivation to learn. In a sense, what is missing is an element of self-exploration, taking knowledge and making it one's own. Ideally, the expertise of the teacher should become intermingled with the goals and achievements of the student. Eisner, a world-renowned researcher on education, coined the term expressive objectives to describe this style of education (Eisner, 1969, p. 15):

> An expressive objective describes an educational encounter; it identifies a situation in which children are to work, a problem with which they are to cope, a task in which they are to engage; but it does not specify what they are to learn from that encounter, situation, problem or task. An expressive objective provides both the teacher and the student with an invitation to explore, defer or focus on issues that are of peculiar interest or import to the inquirer... to serve as a theme around which skills and understandings learned earlier can be brought to bear [and] expanded, elaborated, and made idiosyncratic. With an expressive objective, what is desired is not homogeneity of response among students but diversity.[37,46]

[37,46] Inquiry attempts to reduce the level of pedagogical teaching in favour of a student-driven or cooperative educational encounter. Although increased choice in one's own education may be appealing, is it enjoyed by students in reality? To explore the student

Box 1.3
Styles of Learning: A Complex Issue

In preparation for an in-house presentation of our research, our Inquiry Team wanted to set up an activity to demonstrate that knowledge retention is more effective if students have an active rather than passive role in their learning. We prepared a mini-lecture taken from a description of giraffes found in an actual zoo, detailing aspects of the animal such as its physical appearance, behaviour, and so on. Following the mini-lecture, we wanted to give a short quiz with questions that we felt were representative of the style of tests given in a lecture-based classroom, rewarding students based on how attentively they absorbed the presented facts. We tried this activity on ourselves and although the majority of us felt distanced by the lecture, to our surprise, some members of the Inquiry Team thrived in this learning environment! How could this be?

What we learned from the experience is that choosing the "best" way to learn is complicated; different students will naturally perform optimally in different environments. It also helped us reevaluate why Inquiry-based learning is important. Rather than it being the "best" way for everyone, we began to understand it as an alternative. It provides a learning opportunity for those students who do not fit into a classroom based on traditional pedagogy.

The Imprint of Society on Our Education System

Fortunately, most schools today do not implement the ideologies of traditional pedagogy to a tee. It is inarguable, however, that the constrained views of this paradigm still greatly influence daily practice in our schools. With the recent rise in standardized testing, increased emphasis on grades and rubrics, and the heightening pressures placed on students to absorb a wealth of information, traditional pedagogy's grip on education appears to be growing stronger.

Why is traditional pedagogy favoured by our education system? There is no clear answer to this question. Throughout history, numerous social pressures have tipped the balance of education from being student-centred to teacher-centred, and from promoting individualization to socialization. We will be unable to explore this interesting topic fully in this book, but we would encourage you to do some research on your own. The following are just a few factors that have brought traditional pedagogy to the forefront of education:

experience with increased educational freedom, read more on page 37. The role of an Inquiry instructor differs greatly from that of a lecturer. What are the goals of an Inquiry facilitator? How does an Inquiry instructor conduct a session and communicate with his or her students. Explore this topic further on page 46.

Box 1.4

The coupling of educational institutions and the State

At one time, an educational institution was not much more than a travelling band of renowned scholars who migrated from city to city, settling at wherever they received the most benefits in return for their educational services. During this time, education was relatively independent from the control of the State. However, over time, the State provided increased resources, formal buildings, research equipment, and guaranteed capital, to educational institutions, thereby "locking" them in place. As the educational institutions and the State became increasingly interdependent, there also arose greater restrictions on what was taught. This was a major factor in why schools became institutions for socialization, and places where the interests of the ruling elite could be safeguarded (Haskins, 1923). Even now, external pressures from government curricula and corporate expectations present numerous challenges to a student-centred approach to learning. For example, many teachers who promote a constructivist approach to learning have reported difficulties in allowing students to explore their interests while meeting curriculum expectations (Deboer, 2002).

The challenges of mass education in modern society

Following World War II, the number of undergraduates in the United States rose from two hundred thousand to 1.4 million students. Since that time, enrolment in higher education has observed an approximate ten-fold increase (Falvey, 1996). This surge in the student population has spurred a shift in teaching strategies, the most prominent being the introduction of lecture-based teaching (Falvey, 1996). With increasing numbers of students, it becomes challenging for education to remain an individualized experience.

Consumerism's impact on education

According to education experts such as Alfie Kohn and Stephen Brookfield (2000), education today is under the influence of many corporate interests. Kohn (2004) has commented on how schools are becoming miniaturized business environments, driven by a spirit of competitiveness that pits students against each other. Even when students work in groups, it is usually in the context of defeating another group. Importantly, the "market-driven" classroom deemphasizes the importance of education as a means of building a democratic society. Modern education places greater emphasis on obedience than on self-direction and the development of problem solving skills (Kohn, 2004). Similarly, Brookfield has criticized the use of rewards and punishments that enforce the authority of teachers. Teacher-centred learning results in the affirmation of *hegemony*, a framework of social ideologies favouring a ruling minority that is accepted to be natural, but is based on assumptions that should be questioned (Brookfield, 1993). Hegemony can be seen in the way that terms associated with the marketplace have crept into our schools. We often hear statements like 'the education of our children is an "investment"', 'my child receives "competitive" marks', or 'grades are becoming "inflated"'. All of these ideas persist without much questioning. After all, we send our children to school to prepare them for the business world. What other reason for education could there be?

Take a moment to reflect on these reasons. What are your thoughts? What other reasons might be contributing to the shift towards a teacher-centred education?

Current Needs: The Times They are A-Changin'

What do people today expect to achieve through education? What do we want in the leaders of our society? The general public has expectations of what colleges and universities should provide to students and society. The public desires graduates who are productive and caring members of society and leaders who improve the quality of life of others. The primary focus in undergraduate education is to develop skills in computation, clear written expression, and critical thinking (Zeszotarski, 1999). Employers also have their own expectations concerning what skills and knowledge ideal students should possess. Instead of specific technical skills, most employers prefer that their employees have practical academic and communication skills that enable quick adaptations to new situations. Thus, there should be an emphasis on the development of transferable skills that are necessary in both the workforce and in life. These skills enable graduates to succeed in an ever-changing society (Zeszotarski, 1999).

Can traditional pedagogy foster the development of the kind of leaders and bright, responsible members of society we desire? Unfortunately, based on research, what occurs in a traditional classroom does not coincide with how active learning happens. Active learning involves thinking about the meaning of information, appraising its accuracy, and relating it to what is already known, the net result is increased understanding as well as better recall and retention of information (Fisher & Craik, 1977). By receiving pre-organized information, as is the case in traditional pedagogy, students may gain a sense of familiarity with the information but may find it difficult to apply to real-life situations (Brown, Collins, & Duguid, 1989).

How can improvements be made? First, knowledge should be presented in a realistic context. How we learn influences how we retrieve information at a later time. If information is stored in the absence of a real world context, it is unlikely to be retrieved later in relevant situations. For example, Miller and Gildea (1987) (as cited in Brown, Collins, & Dugoid, 1989) reported that students who learned a new language by memorizing from a dictionary showed inappropriate applications of words and demonstrated slower language acquisition compared to students who acquired the language by experience. In contrast to traditional pedagogy, if learning were to take a constructivist approach, whereby students actively gather information and continuously integrate it into their own personalized knowledge frameworks, information can be stored in a meaningful way (Gray, 1997). Overall, this type of learning fosters the increased knowledge transferability and critical thinking skills that is so highly regarded in our society.

The reshaping of the teacher-student hierarchy may also help produce better learners. One major challenge faced by teachers is the apathetic student, who finds trouble fitting into school. According to some critics, the introduction of standardized tests has distanced these students further as schools are increasingly becoming an institution for the elite, where competition is designed to filter out struggling students. The very notion that this sort of system is justified is again evidence of the hegemony precipitated by our market-driven society (Kohn, 2004). Recent studies have examined factors that influence student persistence in schools (Castles, 2004). An emerging theme is that the school environment helps students cope with stress associated with learning and helps improve self-esteem and motivation. It is not difficult to imagine that a student-centred approach, where teachers are responsive to a student's needs and emotional well-being, would benefit those who are falling behind. Additionally, by acting as model active learners, teachers can exemplify positive ways of coping with stress. The greatest lesson that a teacher can deliver to a student is the passion of learning itself, one that cannot be taught in textbooks or by giving standardized tests. It is a value developed by the student's own inner desire and nourished by the patience of the teacher.

With the changing needs of society, our current model of traditional pedagogy just doesn't seem to offer what we expect from our students. We want leaders who can creatively tackle problems from multiple perspectives, yet our education system awards students who can best follow instructions passively. The bottom line is that we are faced with a gap between what goes on in a teacher-centred classroom and what research tells us about active learning. Likewise, there is a disparity between our own values and those inherent in the model of traditional pedagogy. So what is keeping us from challenging the way things are in education?

Box 1.5

Meeting the Standards

Learning that is driven by an intrinsic desire for self-development. The abolishment of standardized testing. Education where students have input on their own evaluation. Isn't it all a bit too idealistic? (Perhaps, you may be even wondering, *what is the world coming to?*) Is this approach to learning sufficiently rigorous to prepare students for a competitive marketplace?

In the United States, and increasingly in Canada, there is often talk of the "bar" not being set high enough for students. We worry about "inflated" grades that can no longer separate the weak from the strong students. We hear reports that students are "slipping through the cracks," graduating without actually acquiring sufficient knowledge and skills (Rosovsky, 2004). To solve these problems, many education boards have turned towards standardized testing, hoping to measure performance in a non-biased and accountable way. With standardized tests, students are evaluated relative to one another, the proverbial "bell curve" (Kohn, 2004). Correspondingly, there has been a movement away from student-centred learning, viewed by some to be "too soft."

Rather than discussing the pitfalls of standardized testing, a topic thoroughly explored in Kohn, 2004, let us turn to the question of whether *any* method of evaluation is truly effective in predicting future success. What are the characteristics of an ideal evaluation? What kind of test or assignment could you design to accurately measure one's abilities? What challenges would you face in constructing this evaluation?

You might be surprised to learn that many of our most rigorous tests are in reality poor predictors of future performance. For example, a study by Julian (2005) showed the MCAT, used for determining medical school admission, is able to explain only 30% of the variance in medical school GPA, and only 38% of the variance on scores in the United States Medical Licensing Exam (Julian, 2005).

If every student learns differently, how can we construct an evaluation tha takes this variability into account? Without a way of accurately assessing performance, is it right to use standardized tests to judge the fate of students? More fundamentally, we should ask, what is the purpose of evaluation?

Student-centred learning sees evaluation as simply another step in the learning process. It is not about judgment but about monitoring one's process. Interestingly, in universities that provided extra assistance to those who scored lower on the MCAT, Julian (2005) found little relationship between MCAT scores and student performance in medical school. Rather than using grades as cut-offs, maybe they should be used to identify and work on our weaknesses? What do you think?

A Time for Change

Take a moment to reflect upon the various learning environments you have encountered. Which one was most beneficial to your learning? Which one(s) do you feel hindered your learning? If you could devise an educational system, what would it be like?

In recent years, several emerging models of learning and teaching have attempted to realign our education system with our own changing values of what it means to be an educated, productive member of society. Promoted under many different names, androgogy, problem-based learning (PBL), self-directed learning (SDL), experiential learning, and constructivist learning, these models share the common belief that the student should play a more active role in his or her education, directly challenging the teacher-centred approach of traditional pedagogy. As referenced earlier, these theories are in fact not as radical as they first seem; many school systems from another time and place have promoted a student-centred, holistic learning approach. In many ways, *these* "new" ways of learning are actually very old, even more rooted in tradition than what we now associate with a "traditional" lecture-based classroom. Simply, they are radical to us only because they clash with our *perceptions* of what education is, as *we* have experienced it.

Box 1.6
Paradigm Shifts in Undergraduate Education

"The only constant is change"

The financial costs of higher education are continually increasing and students, parents, and taxpayers are becoming concerned that the large public investment into educational resources is not resulting in the desired benefits (Fincher, 1991). According to Doig & Werner (2000), our current pedagogical model is not adequately preparing undergraduates for their futures. A model that focuses on skills and lifelong learning is required to satisfy society's demands for critical thinkers to lead our society. Instead of focusing on what to teach in schools, schools need to focus on how to teach skills that foster lifelong learning and student satisfaction.

Despite the tendencies of educators and institutions to cling to the practices and philosophies of traditional pedagogy, a vocal body of researchers and educators with a vision for the application of innovative learning techniques and philosophies does exist. The philosophies and ideals of such educators are increasingly appearing in academic journals and are being demonstrated through innovative teaching techniques at a select number of educational institutions throughout the world.

Numerous literary works have been published emphasizing the dire need for institutional change in undergraduate education. Among this growing database of information, an article written in 1995 by Robert Barr and John Tagg continues to stand out as a leading and innovative paper. Published in *Change* magazine, a popular education periodical, the article discusses a number of ideas that have generated a revolutionary milestone in scholarly circles, making it the most frequently cited article in the history of the magazine (Barr, Doberneck, Fear, Petrulis, Robinson, & Van Den Berg, 2003). The popularity of the article lies in Barr's and Tagg's vivid presentation of a vision for the future of higher education, urging for a shift from the current Instructional Paradigm.

According to Barr & Tagg, North American higher education has historically existed under the Instructional Paradigm, whereby a college exists to provide instruction and focuses upon methods such as lecturing as opposed to concentrating on learning experiences. The innovative Learning Paradigm is defined as the systematic effort to "create environments and experiences that bring students to discover and construct knowledge for themselves, to make students members of communities of learners that make discoveries and solve problems, and to create a series of ever more powerful learning environments" (Barr & Tagg, 1995, p. 4; Barr et al., 2003, p. 161).

The Learning Paradigm is slowly emerging and becoming accepted in educational institutions, thereby profoundly "chang[ing] everything in education as we know it" (Barr et al., 2003, p. 152). Barr and Tagg assert that under the Instructional Paradigm, colleges and universities have created the guise of a complex educational structure, which in reality primarily exists for the delivery of knowledge and instruction in the form of fifty-minute lectures. In order to see the advantages of this method of learning, institutions are encouraged to shed the assumption that the Instructional Paradigm is supreme simply because of its popular use over time. Operating under the philosophy of the Instructional Paradigm, the main goal of colleges and universities is the provision of instruction, which is comparable to believing that the main goal of a car manufacturer is to operate assembly lines or that the purpose of health care workers is to fill hospital beds (Barr et al., 2003). The Learning Paradigm, which emphasizes student learning as the central goal, is analogous to the goal of car manufacturers to produce high-quality cars and the goal of health care workers to prevent and cure ailments and illness. Educators should understand the importance of providing facilitation to encourage learning through methods that have proven to enhance students' achievement of individual objectives. The Learning Paradigm envisions the institution itself as a learner that will develop and improve over time (Barr & Tagg, 1995). Unfortunately, in a society that continues to embrace traditional pedagogy, such an elegant vision of a utopian learning society brings with it a number of skeptics. The applicability of the Learning Paradigm is scrutinized by critics of Barr and Tagg's article.

The ideas presented by Barr and Tagg are nothing new. You do not have to look far to obtain several articles advocating the use of a Learner Centered Design (LCD) (Barr et al., 2003). The distinguishing feature of Barr and Tagg's article is that it provides a framework for the application of the Learning Paradigm to institutions. In fact, the most compelling outcome explored in the work of Barr and Tagg is the belief that "there is no final answer for what works best to enable students to learn deeply and for colleges and universities to get better at what they do over time" (Barr & Tagg, 2005, p. 163). In asserting that one method or idea is better, the potential shift from teaching to learning is constrained by preventing the exploration of additional options in order to continue the development and improvement of the educational system. We have all learned that there is no right or wrong way to learn, and as such, it only makes sense that there is not one preferred way for educators and institutions to nurture the learning process.

How do these emerging models differ from traditional pedagogy? The first diversion concerns the reasoning behind why we learn. In contrast to traditional pedagogy, the emerging models see education as having the purpose of enriching our experiences as people, helping us learn not only about our world but also about ourselves. There is more to learning than simply becoming productive employees; education is the path to purposeful living. Humanistic psychologists, such as Carl Rogers and Abraham Maslow, promote the idea that people continuously strive toward self-actualization (the act of realizing one's potential in life). Self-actualization is not a static state, but one that is constantly changing, just as one's perception of his or her identity changes with time. It is indistinguishable from an understanding of self. Individuals move toward self-actualization through new discoveries about who they are in the context of the world around them. Thus, education should help people to continuously uncover what they desire while providing them with the tools and motivations to undertake their unique journeys in life (Huitt, 2001).

A second area of contrast to traditional education is the emphasis on a problem-based approach to learning. Under this model, individual students take the initiative (sometimes in the context of a group) to diagnose their own needs, formulate their own goals, and determine their own learning strategies. Subscribers to the student-directed approach have the potential to reap many benefits from the process. These include the possibility of greater retention, understanding, and application of the knowledge learned. Learners have been found to initiate learning with a greater sense of purpose and motivation, as this approach gives the opportunity for students to manage new situations independently. It creates a sense of confidence, and further develops personal life skills such as responsibility and accountability (Levett-Jones, 2005).

Finally, under the emerging views of education, learning is perceived as a dynamic process that can take numerous forms, from reading to doing, and from self-study to interaction with others. Particularly, experiential learning is placed in high regard due to the influence of humanistic values. How we learn from everyday experiences should not be discounted and acquired knowledge should be a reflection of these experiences whenever possible. What we learn inside a classroom should not be isolated from what goes on outside the walls of our schools. In this way, the knowledge that we gain has a context to something that is important to us personally. Think about the learning that goes on in your own life. As the Chinese proverb goes, "I hear and I forget, I see and I remember, I do and I understand."

Would you agree that the knowledge that has stayed with you and influenced you the most was acquired through meaningful and personal experiences? Take a few minutes to think about whether you agree or disagree with this statement.

Box 1.7
Struggling with Self-direction

SDL can understandably be a frustrating experience for students (Levett-Jones, 2005). Real-life problems are not as straightforward as the well-thought-out tests with predetermined answers that we find in traditional class-rooms. It is arduous to navigate through uncharted waters with boundless paths and destinations. Several barriers have impeded the application of SDL in undergraduate programs. Since students come from years of traditional teacher-led learning, it may be difficult to accept SDL and employ its principles. Frustration comes as a result of the lack of skills required for self-direction. These frustrations are often targeted toward the facilitator who does not fulfill a traditional role. To make matters more difficult, SDL can be implemented in the classroom inappropriately. For example, by placing time constraints and specific content requirements to make SDL more practical, students are faced with conflicting messages, a dissonance of expectations from two very different paradigms (Levett-Jones, 2005). Students can also have false perceptions of SDL, developing a sense that they are free to learn (and not learn) whatever topics they please (Norman, 1999). Students should be made aware of the distinction that their own individuality, preferences, and goals are to complement and enhance an established curriculum. They do not form it. Or in other words:

Student-centred learning] does not mean that student preferences drive the problem selection in a problem-based curriculum. Rather, it means that adult learners have some or all of the necessary characteristics to engage in self-directed learning and that this ability should be fostered by faculty" (Macdonald, 1991, p. 110).

The self-direction of students should be regulated through a balance of self-evaluation and feedback from facilitators and tutors, so that students acquire a sufficient amount of fundamental knowledge (Vaughn, Baker, Dewitt, 2000; Rangachari, 2004; Rangachari, 1991).

There are certainly many reasons why we should adopt a new learning paradigm adhering to the principles and visions we have just discussed. All these reasons can be embraced by our need to become lifelong learners in our ever-changing world. What is lifelong learning anyway? While people need certain skills to be effective lifelong learners, at the root of this notion is a distinctive attitude, a set of core beliefs that drive people to explore the world. According to Gentle (2001), planting the seeds of these beliefs is a responsibility of educational institutions, and they can most effectively carry out this task by shaping the culture of the learning environment and by establishing the way that interpersonal relationships are viewed. The culture of exploration is exemplified in creating a collaborative environment and establishing the idea that teachers, students, and those outside of the formal educational institution can actively learn from each other. In this environment, individuals continuously learn, appraise, and incorporate the views of others (Bolhuis, 2003).

Before moving on to the next section, take some time and reflect on the following quotation that summarizes the need for our society to change its views about education.

> We are, in my view, faced with an entirely new situation in education where the goal of education if we are to survive, is the facilitation of change and learning. The only [person] who is educated is the [one] who has learned how to learn, the [one] that has realized that no knowledge is secure, that only the process of seeking knowledge gives a basis for security (Levett-Jones, 2005, p. 364).

What do you think?

How Inquiry Satisfies Needs

As a reader, a shift in perspective is required in order to appreciate this book. It is a move that is perhaps difficult, requiring courage and faith. It is a drift from the comfort developed from years of learning, and living, under the instructions of an "all-knowing" teacher. The ways that we have lived have shaped our values. It is difficult to question these values, for doing so leads us to challenge not only our authorities but ourselves as well. You are not alone with your feelings and fears. The authors of this book, and our peers in the Bachelor of Health Sciences Program at McMaster University, have all felt these fears and frustrations. The lines between educators and students are becoming increasingly blurred. We are all learners. It is our responsibility to search for ways to challenge the status quo and to question our assumptions about what it means to learn. Our efforts have blossomed and continue to grow into truly promising alternatives to learning that help enrich our lives.[27,37]

[27,37] To see a description of the BHSc philosophy and how it attempts to address learning needs, turn to page 27. To explore the students' opinions of the Inquiry method in the BHSc program, turn to page 37.

Topic 2: Inquiry in the
Bachelor of Health Sciences Program

[6] It was the morning of September 13, 2005 when we first met as a group. As we walked into our meeting room, our minds were overflowing with questions about this mysterious course called "The Inquiry Book Project." We knew that we had to write a book. We knew there were 14 of us along with a facilitator. We knew we had one year to do it. But there were so many unanswered questions: Why were we writing a book? What questions were we looking to answer? Where do we begin? Could it even be done? Yet, here we are today. How did we get here? The answer is: Inquiry.[113]

Inquiry: Its Principles and Methods

[99] Here is a challenge for you. Plan a trip to somewhere you've never been before.

---

[6] You are here because you wished to learn more about alternatives to traditional lecture-based teaching methods. This section will show you how we "kick it," *Inquiry*-style! As you are reading, why not jot down some comparisons between Inquiry and the traditional classroom. What learning advantages does Inquiry offer? Is there anything about Inquiry which makes you uncomfortable?

[113] If you would like to further explore our journey, turn to "Methodology & Our Experience" on page 113.

[99] After completing this exercise you can continue reading about group work on page 99 or you may choose to further explore the nature of Inquiry by continuing to read page 24.

The Inquiry model is innovative in the sense that it challenges the conventional, content-focused curriculum found in today's schools. Yet, you may be surprised to know that the Inquiry process is not new. In fact, as humans, we are all natural Inquiry learners.

Consider the challenge we just presented to you. How did you solve the problem? Perhaps, the first thing you did was ask, "Where would I go?" Maybe even before this question, you first wondered, "Why am I being given this challenge?" or "How do I answer this?" Inquiry begins by asking questions. Before you seek an answer, you have to first identify and understand the problem. Next, you would seek ways to answer your questions. You might search on the Internet or ask a friend for suggestions of places to visit. From each resource, you obtain information that you then appraise for accuracy and applicability to your question. If you asked your friend where it is you should go, and he or she gave you instructions for airline discounts, you might choose another resource. What you learned did not answer your original question but raised new ones, instead. Eventually, you incorporate information gathered from numerous resources to construct an overall picture. At this point, you would evaluate if your question has been answered. If it hasn't, you go back to an earlier step, perhaps posing a new question or seeking more resources. ↪46

99,101,112,131↘ The method of problem solving above describes the Inquiry process, which can be more formally represented by the IREC model (see Figure 2.1).

↪46 Facilitators guide the Inquiry process. To see the role of the facilitator in helping students to think on their own, turn to page 46.

99, 112,131↘ Read on to understand the Inquiry process.

Fig. 2.1

The Inquiry Process

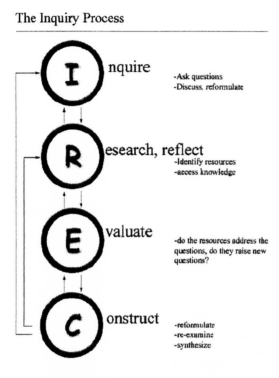

I nquire
-Ask questions
-Discuss, reformulate

R esearch, reflect
-Identify resources
-access knowledge

E valuate
-do the resources address the questions, do they raise new questions?

C onstruct
-reformulate
-re-examine
-synthesize

Elements from IREC and the Inquiry philosophy can often be found in the literature on education. For example, in the Cyclical Model of the Learning Process proposed by Kolb, reflection is one of the four key elements in intellectual development (Thorpe, 2000). Kolb's model also emphasizes that the Learning Process occurs in daily life, not just in formal academic settings.

Despite our innate tendency to practice Inquiry, academic institutions often discourage it from taking place. For example, tests and assignments constructed solely by the instructor can limit the time available for students to ask their own questions and explore their own interests. Also in traditional classrooms, more emphasis is placed on the memorization of isolated facts than on the development of skills that help produce effective learning (Gibbs & Coffey, 2004).

Inquiry is a process that encourages skills development and holistic knowledge acquisition. Most importantly, it cultivates lifelong learning and promotes a multi-faceted approach towards pursuing life's opportunities. The essence of Inquiry cannot be generalized; the Inquiry experience and what it means is as unique as the individual.

Inquiry Skills

The skills developed in Inquiry are valuable largely for their transferability. They become assets not only in academia, but also in real-life, at home and at work. For instance, the ability to work as a team and to critically analyze situations is just as important in the home as it is at the office. It is the goal of the BHSc Program to develop life-long learning skills with Inquiry, through different projects and activities.

Box 2.1 [84,96]

The BHSc Skill Set

1. Time management - setting priorities, managing time and staying on track
2. Posing a good question and refining it
3. Identifying sources of information - libraries, online indices, World Wide Web and experts
4. Evaluating (critical thinking) and integrating information
5. Using information to answer a question
6. Communication skills - verbal, nonverbal, and written
7. Working with other people
   a. Identifying individual and group strengths and weaknesses
   b. Dividing responsibility
   c. Following through
   d. Teaching each other and learning from each other
   e. Giving and receiving constructive feedback
   f. Dealing with minor conflict
8. Evaluating strengths and weaknesses in each of the above areas [60]

Eventually, these skills are gauged and acknowledged by a set of student-facilitator interviews, in contrast to traditional evaluations like written tests. This way, hindrances or gaps in the learning process can be recognized and appropriate feedback can be given to the student.[65] Furthermore, as one Inquiry facilitator would frequently emphasize, "Inquiry is all about examining the breadth, depth and application of the issue at hand." Contemplating solutions for a problem is very similar to an architect envisioning a building design. The eventual appearance of the architect's building can take on an infinite number of forms,

---

[84,96] Read the core skills of BHSc., the development of which is fostered by the culture.

[60] The skill set listed in the box above is core to the philosophy of the BHSc Program, and the development of these skills is one of the central objectives of Inquiry courses. To hear students' stories about the different skills students develop in Inquiry, turn to Section 3.3, "Skill Development", on page 60.

[65] What is this peer evaluation all about? How does it fit with the philosophy of Inquiry? Turn to page 65 to find out!

but the building will not stand without a strong, concrete foundation. Likewise, the solution to a problem may take on an infinite number of forms, but there should always be a solid problem-solving framework at the base of this solution. Improving this problem-solving framework is what Inquiry attempts to achieve.

Origins and Philosophy of the Bachelor of Health Sciences Program

[21] It is the early 1990s and you are a second year student at McMaster. You have heard that one of your courses is not easy. You are expecting plenty of reading, memorization, and difficult tests. Your anxiety is particularly high though, because you have heard rumours that there is a new professor teaching the course, and that he has completely overhauled the curriculum. The course is now being taught in similar ways to courses offered by the McMaster medical school. Additionally, you see the terms "Problem-Based Learning" and "Inquiry" mentioned a lot in the course outline, which just adds to your confusion, as you do not really know what these terms mean. Your friend who took the course last year mentioned the class was small, only about 40 people, which is why you are surprised when you walk in and almost 100 boisterous students are crammed into the lecture hall. A man walks into the classroom welcoming you to the beginnings of Inquiry in a non-professional, undergraduate course.

It was not until 1999 that the Inquiry method of learning was formalized into an undergraduate program. In the late 1990s, McMaster University began to increase its focus on research innovation, and part of this increased focus included a call for proposals from each faculty. One of the conditions for submitting a proposal was that it needed to be accompanied by a plan to create a new undergraduate program. A group of professors within the Faculty of Health Sciences envisioned a program that would give students an interdisciplinary education.

Despite the larger roles that some individuals played in the development of Inquiry, many of the original facilitators will agree that although individual vision and labour were important, faculty collaboration was the key to the program's success. Numerous other individuals and groups were involved in the steps leading up to the creation of the BHSc Program.

Box 2.2

The Mind Behind the BHSc

Many of the concepts of Inquiry within the BHSc Program have been developed by a research scientist at McMaster University. He had been exposed to Inquiry for most of his educational career, as a graduate student, as a researcher,

---

[21] BHSc: is it the alternative for enhancing our learning as instructors and students? Read on to find out for yourself.

and finally as a teacher. At first, he only taught graduate students, medical students and residents. Then, in the early 1990s, he began teaching non-professional undergraduate students. After teaching with the traditional didactic method, an attempt was made to turn a traditionally lecture-based course into a unique PBL experience. Improvements were incorporated into the marking schemes and a feedback system between the students and the instructors was implemented. Communication between faculty and students was then improved with the use of an interactive, online discussion forum, entitled The Little Red School House or LearnLink. LearnLink added one more level of engagement and interaction to the course, and has expanded to become part of other courses since then.[106,93]

Within a few years of the course redesign, the enrolment ballooned from 45 to 180 students. Soon similar undergraduate science courses were reinvented, followed by similar results (D. Harnish, personal communication, January 23, 2006). These early pioneering initiatives were of great help to the eventual establishment of the BHSc Program.

From the onset, the BHSc Program was to have Inquiry-based courses at its core, flanked by more traditional courses of psychobiology, statistics, and a selection of electives. Inquiry is unique in the sense that it is not taught by professors; rather, it is a process guided by 'facilitators'. It was expected that facilitators would face challenges when introducing Inquiry to students inexperienced with this new style of learning. Thus, professors of the highest calibre were sought. With word spreading of the new BHSc Program, it did not take long for professors to come looking for teaching opportunities (D. Harnish, personal communication, January 23, 2006). Professors who had never taught undergraduates were coming forward, hoping to become Inquiry facilitators in the new program (S. Barrett, personal communication, January 10, 2006).

When the first class of the BHSc Program arrived at McMaster in September of 1999, they were in for an experience like no other. The Inquiry classes were venturing into new territory, and no one was quite sure how it would turn out. At first, it was proposed that the BHSc Program offer courses based on the four pillars of the Canadian Institute for Health Research: biomedicine, population health, applied clinical practice, and health systems (CIHR, 2004). This proposal was later rejected, and instead, it was decided that the BHSc Program would allow students to experience the health sciences as a Complex-Adaptive System, rather than just a collection of regimented courses. This model allowed for more flexibility, and it was congruent with the innovative and interdisciplinary style that the administration was trying to achieve (Zimmerman, 1998).

[106,93] What is this LearnLink all about? Turn to page 106 to find out how this computer software acts as a resource for student learning. Are you curious to learn about other learning resources in the BHSc Program? If so, turn to page 93.

Box 2.3

Complex-Adaptive Systems

A Complex-Adaptive System (CAS) is, quite simply, exactly what it sounds like. It is a way of examining and considering how an entity functions, whether it is an ecosystem, a human body, or a university program. A key concept is that there is an intricate and dense network of connections and relationships between all of the individual parts of the entity. As well, these parts are varied and diverse, and can change over time. In a CAS, it is not the individual parts that are most important in determining how the entity works, but the relationships between these individual parts. In a CAS, there is no one single piece or person in charge, all the smaller parts have a portion of the control. In this sense, the outcomes or products of the system are very unpredictable, especially because adaptation can occur.

The following example of a CAS is given in *Edgeware*, a book that examines these systems in the context of healthcare (Zimmerman, 1998).

> Weather systems are often cited as examples of this phenomenon of nonlinearity. The butterfly effect, a term coined by meteorologist Edward Lorenz, is created, in part, by the huge number of nonlinear interactions in weather. The butterfly effect suggests that sometimes a seemingly insignificant difference can have a huge influence. Lorenz found that in simulated weather forecasting, two almost identical simulations could result in radically different weather patterns. A very tiny change to the initial variables, metaphorically something as small as a butterfly flapping its wings, can radically alter the outcome. The weather system is very sensitive to the initial conditions and to its history. (Zimmerman, 1998, p.11)

The Implementation of Inquiry in the Bachelor of Health Sciences Program

So you are now admitted as a BHSc student. Your next challenge is to figure out what Inquiry encompasses and how it is implemented in the program. How can you excel? What about grades? How will you be evaluated? With Inquiry in the horizon for the next four years, you are confused and worried.

Box 2.4

Prevalent emotions experienced in the first month of Inquiry [37]

---

[37] Emotions are of course, subject to change. Students during the four years of the BHSc. Program experience a spectrum of sentiments, some positive and some negative. To explore some of these emotions and how they impact learning according to students,

• Anxiety	• Uncertainty
• Puzzlement	• Fear
• Anger	• Resentment

YEAR 1

[99,103] HTH SCI 1E06: Inquiry I is a mandatory course listed in your first year student timetable. Having heard the buzz word "Inquiry" in BHSc brochures, on the BHSc website, or when talking to friends, you begin to wonder what it is all about. With anxiety, you enter your class of 15-20 students and are greeted by a facilitator and fourth year peer tutors.[96] The intimate setting and the nature of this course seem like unfamiliar territory. After attending a few sessions, at least one aspect of Inquiry becomes clear to you: it aims to initiate skill development rather than teach a content base. However, the lack of a familiar course outline and evaluation scheme raises your anxiety further. What is more surprising is that that students in different classrooms do not follow a single, preset learning agenda. Each Inquiry classroom is as unique as the learners who shape it.

Near the beginning of the term, it is announced that you are required to have two or more one-on-one interviews over the course of the year with your facilitator. The purpose of these interviews is to evaluate your learning progress and to address prevalent concerns or problems. You have to demonstrate how you have managed to meet your learning objectives and how you have implemented all the skills that were outlined at the beginning of the year.

It takes a while for students to get used to Inquiry. It may take some individuals a month, a semester, or even a year to come to appreciate the Inquiry process, while other individuals may never appreciate the process. The content that a group chooses to explore is less relevant than the development of good collaboration, critical thinking, effective communication, and research skills. Inquiry is learning how to learn, mastering learning skills through practice. The skills learned in Inquiry I help students achieve their future goals.

Monumental by itself, you realize that Inquiry I is complemented by another full year course HTH SCI 1I06: Cellular and Molecular Systems and Practicum in Health Sciences (Biology), which allows for application of Inquiry skills to the study of biology. You are also required to take HTH SCI 1G03: Psychobiology where you learn psychology through a combination of lectures and Inquiry-style group learning.

---

go to page 37 where you can start at the beginning or skip to the emotions you find most interesting.
[99,103] This section provides an overview of major courses offered by the BHSc Program. As you read, pay attention to how these courses help promote collective learning.
[96] The peer tutor is a perplexing and mysterious entity to a first-year Inquiry student. To learn more about the role of peer tutors, turn to page 96.

Box 2.5

Progression vs. Process

In the 2005-2006 school year, all first year students in Inquiry I utilized both the novel *The Curious Incident of the Dog in the Night-time* (Haddon, 2004) and the healthcare issue of autism as triggers to inspire their Inquiry learning. Many different areas of exploration resulted within each facilitator's section and within each smaller Inquiry group. The two triggers inspired various themes and topics of study such as astronomy, bioethics, crime-scene investigation, and teaching models, all of which provided rich opportunities for the first year students to develop their Inquiry skills from diverse directions.

YEAR 2

Marked by anxiety, fluctuating morale, and triumph, first-year Inquiry is a blur in retrospect. Uncertain of how to identify concretely the skills or knowledge acquired in Inquiry I, you feel apprehension towards the second year Inquiry course, HTH SCI 2E03: Inquiry II. After seeking advice and reassurance from upper years, you conceptualize this course to be a continuation of Inquiry I, albeit with a different format. After attending the first class, you learn that this half-year course utilizes a problem-based learning (PBL) format to allow for exploration of a major illness category. In past Inquiry II classes, students have learned about infectious disease, genetic complications, cancer, occupational/environmental health, and obesity. In Inquiry II, you and your peers are divided into groups of 10. Each group is assigned a specific sub-topic and designated a facilitator for further guidance. Aside from bimonthly half-hour meetings with your facilitator, your group is on its own.

Inquiry II offers an ideal platform for the implementation of the skills acquired during Inquiry I. In individual groups, you have to devise a research question, a research strategy, and a timeline. Once you are comfortable with your research question and have confirmed it with your facilitator, you have to start researching the subject. Eventually, your goal is to accomplish the learning objective as stated in the course outline, which may be, for example, to find a cure for a disease. At the end of the semester, you have to write a paper and conduct a presentation of your findings in front of the class. In your group of 10 students, smaller groups are often formed to distribute the large task at hand into smaller, more manageable components. In retrospect, you realize how your time management and organization skills honed in Inquiry I can assist you in your current project. After learning a specific component, such as the topic's biochemical properties, members come back together and teach each other. Throughout this process, group learning and peer teaching flows frequently. The facilitators guide you toward a proper direction and help with difficulties that you may have about the research subject. You contemplate this method, and quietly acknowledge and appreciate the benefits of having endured those personal facilitator interviews in Inquiry I where you were first introduced to this kind of guided learning.

Like Inquiry II, the course HTH SCI 2K03: Cell Biology follows a similar format. Once again, you learn that Inquiry skills are a fundamental part of the class. Unlike first year, where you shuddered at the mention of group work, oral presentation, and collaboration, you find yourself increasingly comfortable and genuinely enthusiastic about these challenges. Although the emphasis in your second year is more product-oriented (group essay and presentation), the continued development of Inquiry skills is still inherent.

Box 2.6

Ideas in Action
Course Objective for HTH SCI 2E03: Inquiry II 2005–2006

You have been recruited by Health Canada to consult on a research project that has been initiated to address the challenges posed by our nation's aging population. You will be assigned a sequence fragment that has emerged from a series of screening experiments using differential display and cDNA array technology. These screens were designed to identify factors that may play a role in the aging process. Each group will be assigned a different sequence fragment to investigate. Your task, as a team, is to determine what the sequence is and how it might   be   involved   in   the   molecular   biology   of   aging.

YEAR 3

In third year, the Inquiry course is HTH SCI 3E03: Inquiry III. Inquiry in third year takes the form of many subsections based on various subjects. In the 2005-2006 school year for example, sections that were offered included: Alzheimer's, Body Mind Spirit, Complex Adaptive Systems, Child Development, Creative Writing, Communication, Immunology, Vaccines, and The Inquiry Book. Of the diverse topics, it is highly recommended that one be chosen based on personal preference. You hear varying opinions on the different course topics, but an overall consensus is that, regardless of the choice, the course will facilitate the extensive application of the skills developed in your past Inquiry experiences.

In third year, there is also HTH SCI 3H03: Inquiry Project. In this third year course, you take a more self-directed role in exploring a topic of interest. You can now apply the skills you have developed to real-life settings by designing an independent project in partnership with a supervisor of your choosing. You hear from upper years and faculty members that many students in the past have even arranged international placements for their projects. You shape your own learning. How do you feel about that?

YEAR 4

In fourth year, the core course is either HTH SCI 4A09: Thesis or its shorter version HTH SCI: 4B06 Senior Project. Both of these courses are similar in format to HTH SCI 3H03: Inquiry Project and are usually completed with the help or supervision from a faculty member. Thesis is a research project that may involve work in a research laboratory as well as writing and defending a formal thesis. Senior Project is an information-based research project that may include a comprehensive study of selected topics accompanied by written reports or oral presentations.

Throughout your entire undergraduate experience, you have been involved in a course entitled HTH SCI 4X03: Collaboration and Peer Tutoring. This course is unique in that it spans all four years. An important part of the BHSc Program is to develop a learning community that incorporates the concepts of collaboration, peer tutoring, and life-long learning. This course encourages these activities both formally and informally. It illustrates the value that your learning is not confined to a classroom, practical experiences are equally valuable. For this course, you are required to complete a yearly Plan of Action that includes learning objectives and methods of achieving those objectives. At the end of each year, you reflect on your progress and receive anonymous feedback from upper year students. The skills to think critically and provide constructive feedback become more cohesive in your mind as you proceed to this last stage of your undergraduate experience.

Box 2.7

BHSc Philosophy

The BHSc Program is based on an innovative and unique learning philosophy that incorporates learning methods developed at McMaster University over the past twenty-five years. It is driven by a variety of principles that have established McMaster's reputation as a leader in education.

1. Interdisciplinary approach: The Health Sciences are not viewed as a group of separate departments and fields, but rather, as a complex interconnected field (Harnish et al., 2005). The BHSc Program employs an interdisciplinary approach to the study of health by offering students courses that highlight biological, behavioural, and demographic perspectives. The program uses a broad range of health departments, which include Medicine, Pathology & Molecular Medicine, Psychiatry

& Behavioural Neurosciences, and Clinical Epidemiology & Biostatistics, to construct its course contents. In this way, students are prepared for a variety of careers including medicine, therapy, rehabilitation, epidemiology, education, or graduate studies (Bachelor of Health Sciences, 2005a).

2. Lifelong Learning: The program operates on the belief that learning is not limited to a semester or to a classroom. It strives to teach students skills that will remain with them for their entire lives, no matter which career they choose. Furthermore, these skills will continue to develop throughout their lives (Harnish et al., 2005).

3. Collaboration: The importance of collaboration and group work cannot be understated. Learning is a dynamic process that is more productive when students are meeting and discussing, instead of sitting in a packed lecture hall. The BHSc Program promotes a learning environment to capture that ideal (Bachelor of Health Sciences, 2005b).

4. Student Empowerment: Students have a large say in how the program and courses are run (Bachelor of Health Sciences, 2005a). The administration takes student concerns and suggestions seriously, and does its best to bring about any recommended changes. For example, each year, current students are recruited to read over and evaluate the supplementary applications of prospective candidates so they can be involved in the shaping of their learning environment (Harnish et al., 2005).

5. Community: The BHSc Program is relatively small compared to other programs at McMaster. As such, students form a tight-knit community (S. Barrett, personal communication, January 10, 2006). They get to know everyone in their classes, they address professors by their first names, and they are encouraged to communicate directly with all the faculty members. This sense of community builds better relationships and creates a setting where everyone is approachable and encouraging (D. Harnish, personal communication, January 23, 2006).

As you embark in your fourth year, you see that students have regular group meetings to work on subjects of their interest. Taking part in different activities in the community throughout all four years also contributes to a student's effort in 4X03. Each year, a student's participation will be evaluated in a number of ways, including reflective journals, online interaction with peer groups, interviews, and participation in public seminars. In these fourth year courses, students take self-directed learning to its highest level. All of the Inquiry skills developed in past years are continually being utilized, enhanced, and refined in various academic and community situations. You recall the time when you first stepped into a small classroom with students seated in a large circle, and of the immense fear and anxiety that overwhelmed you. You chuckle at how much you have progressed in these interweaving four years of Inquiry, and slowly grasp the meaning of it all.

Your personal reflections thus far...

Topic 3: Student Experience with Inquiry

10, 21, 117↘

3.1 Emotions

[91↘30,65,73↘] An individual experiences a variety of positive and negative emotions upon embarking on his or her Inquiry journey. This range of emotions evolves and progresses throughout the journey, possibly ending up in a complete change to the feelings that were initially experienced. The emotional component of the Inquiry experience plays an important role in influencing an individual's learning. Think of how important it is to feel comfortable and confident when writing an examination, or how difficult it may be to complete an assignment when you are overcome with frustration and confusion. At any time, the strong feelings we experience can heavily influence how effectively we learn. In the same way, our emotions can affect our Inquiry journey.

When students begin their very first Inquiry course, its new and unfamiliar structure provides a great deal of confusion and frustration to most of the students. Inquiry challenges the "norms" of education by not providing a course outline or a grading scheme, eliminating tests and exams, and by allowing students, as opposed to teachers, to assume the classroom's directive role and develop the class' focus. This may often result in a sense of insecurity amongst

---

[10, 21, 117↘] You are here to delve into the experiences of students who have been on their own Inquiry journeys.

[91↘] You have just explored the Inquiry culture. The frustrations and joys that come from the Inquiry process bring students closer; their common experiences solidify the sense of community. This section explores the emotional journey of Inquiry.

[30,65,73↘] You are here because you wish to learn more about emotions experienced in the course of Inquiry. Our research tells us that emotions play a big part in student learning. Read on to find out how!

participating students because they feel uncomfortable with an Inquiry-style approach to learning. However, in many cases, when time passes and confusion and insecurity are eased as students become more comfortable with the Inquiry learning method, they may experience feelings of satisfaction and achievement. Take a moment to consider this quotation:

> Inquiry was always a new experience every time you walked into class. It was at times frustrating, at times exciting, at times rewarding, and at the beginning, it was mostly confusing. It is difficult to switch into Inquiry mode [especially] when you are coming from the mindset of a person who enjoys marking schemes, breakdowns, and instructions. It's like before [when] you asked, "How high do you want me to jump?" the teacher would tell you, and you'd get an A. Now you say, "How high should I jump?" and you get, "How high do you think you should jump?" So, you end up jumping as high as you possibly can, never knowing when to stop. It really allows you to accomplish great things.

Think of an achievement in your life of which you are proud. What were the feelings and emotions you experienced throughout the steps you took to achieve this? Could you have made this achievement without the positive or negative emotions you experienced in the process you took to reach your goal? Jot down your thoughts:

This section discusses the various positive and negative emotions that individuals experience during Inquiry. Although this section's focus is on emotions, it is important to note that many other experiences are expressed throughout this entire book.

Frustration and Confusion

[85] Frustration is a common feeling amongst Inquiry students. It often occurs near the beginning of an Inquiry course, but it also transpires at various times throughout the Inquiry journey. Feelings of frustration are closely associated with feelings of confusion. It may be difficult to grasp concepts in Inquiry when shifting from traditional learning methods to Inquiry. For example, it is

---

[85] When do students experience frustration? How do they deal with it?

quite confusing to most students that the process in attaining a goal may be equally or more important than the goal itself, especially considering that the majority of students' past focus was primarily directed on producing a final product, regardless of how it was achieved. Frustration can also arise as students create their own learning objectives. They may worry about not attaining a particular knowledge set as they would in traditional lecture-based teaching. Facilitators and peer tutors inform students that feelings of frustration are anticipated. Although most students become frustrated and confused with Inquiry, there are students who do not perceive this to be an issue. When these few students experience these emotions, they refrain from becoming overwhelmed and trust that the frustration they feel is simply a part of the Inquiry journey.

The quotations below exemplify students' feelings of frustration and confusion with Inquiry:

Initially, I had no idea what was going on. Again, I was wondering, "Where is the curriculum, where is the textbook"? And the facilitator kept saying there was no curriculum, you choose whatever project you want and you can get anything you want out of this class. There is no critical thing you have to learn from it, just what you have to learn from it, just what you want from it. And again, it's just the structure issue. We had so much structure in high school.

I hated the first semester of first year Inquiry. I found it pointless and disappointing. The first couple of weeks I felt that I was not learning anything and that the 3 hours spent during class could be devoted to other more reasonable, beneficial causes. I hated the lack of direction and structure that the course offered. I have never been thrown into a situation where I had to discover how to manage my time, make my own decisions, acquire evidence, and find relevant resources on my own. I did not know what to expect from the course and what I had to accomplish in order to get a decent grade in the course. But that was the problem. I was [so] grade-oriented that I did not see what the course was trying to accomplish, how to collaborate in groups, and learn actively through self-motivation. [I] felt that the facilitator and peer tutors saw that I was struggling but were not doing anything about it. I was even contemplating dropping out of the program at the end of first semester because I found Inquiry so frustrating.

I don't think I was mad or anything, but it was frustrating. But I don't think I had a huge problem with it because I wasn't the only one that felt that way. If I was sitting there being really out of the loop, that would've made me panic a little bit, but everyone was the same way so it made me think that this is the way it's supposed to be. And even our peer tutors reinforced that we will be confused and frustrated, and that it was supposed to be that way. (...) That was very reassuring so I wasn't so emotionally stressed or angry or anything like that. It was more like, "Okay, this is how it's supposed to be. I'm a little confused, but we'll get there."

To quote [a facilitator], "Learning is a messy business that requires an individual to become comfortable with being uncomfortable." Inquiry has shown me that learning is a process that is fraught with frustration and failure. Inquiry has presented me with many challenges that have knocked me off my feet. I now know it is my responsibility to pick myself up. As such, my experience of Inquiry has been analogous [to] learning to walk.

The emotional experience associated with Inquiry is a rollercoaster ride that is essential in order to fully understand and appreciate the learning benefits Inquiry provides. Feelings of frustration often exist because Inquiry facilitators take a more passive role in the classroom, leaving students in control of the class' direction. Imagine a teacher coming to class and assigning a project with the only guideline being that there is no guideline; the project can be on any topic you desire and presented in whichever format you choose. It is easy to see how this self-directed approach to learning can be overwhelming and confusing, as it is often something that students will have never experienced before. However, if facilitators were to take a more active role in the classroom and offer direction to their students in an effort to ease frustrations, students may have difficulty in truly understanding self-directed learning and be unable to develop the necessary skills required to perform[46, 135], as exemplified in the quotation below.

> I mean at first I didn't understand the role of the facilitator. I was like, "Why do they never tell us anything and why do they keep bouncing questions back at us?" I was very confused. I guess that's why I didn't speak up. I was very intimidated. I understand now, because it makes you go and look for it yourself. If you look for it yourself, you're going to remember it better than if someone just tells you the answer. If you actually have to think about what you're doing, I think it makes a much deeper impression on you. At first I don't think I saw any merit in it, but slowly, very slowly, it helped.

Comfort

From a student's first Inquiry course to the rest of his or her Inquiry experiences, several other emotions rise and fall, intensify and diminish, in various patterns. These feelings can include fear, confidence, and nervousness in addition to many others. The frustration and confusion, which existed in initial experiences, also exist in future Inquiry projects, but the added benefit of being more comfortable and confident with the Inquiry philosophy may be able to ease the frustration and confusion that students experience. Students are comforted with the idea that they have experienced it before and they trust that it will work again. This sense of familiarity with Inquiry develops as students spend more time in Inquiry-based settings. Once students lose the insecurities they have about Inquiry, they can often understand and appreciate the learning benefits that Inquiry has to offer. This is analogous to many things that people learn in

---

[46, 135] Facilitators serve as important figures in self-directed learning. How does a facilitator help BHSc students develop independence? If you are interested in this question, read more on page 46. Feelings of frustration are integral to the Inquiry experience. How have frustrations played a part in the Inquiry Book project? Turn to page 135 to find out!

their lives. Think back to when you learned to ride a bike. The initial times you practiced riding without training wheels may have been frustrating, discouraging, and even painful. However, over time, with practice and experience, a sense of comfort developed and you realized how great bike riding can be. Through this, you can appreciate that you needed to struggle in order to be successful and to truly see the benefits of your achievement. Developing comfort with Inquiry is no different.

Reflect on this quotation in which a student explains their development of comfort with the Inquiry process:

> I think [there is] a point where you become more comfortable with the whole process. It seems less foreign, less, "Okay, what's happening now?" You get used to always feeling that tiny bit of lost but you know that that's okay, and that you will find which way you want to go and find the answer to [your] question. [It was] probably just when we got to doing more [Inquiry journals and presentations], just settling down in Inquiry, and just everything started to fit together. [You think], "Okay this isn't bad, [and] sort of keep going."

Learning is often positively affected by being more comfortable with Inquiry as a method of learning. As comfort progresses with continued experience, a new learning environment is developed. In addition, students are more familiar and often more comfortable with elements, such as group work, that are associated with Inquiry. The newly acquired comfort can foster better learning for some students. However, there are students who do not find comfort necessary and a few cases in which comfort hindered learning.

These examples highlight some students' experiences with comfort development in relation to establishing a new learning environment and to group work:

> In lecture courses I usually don't speak up. [Professors] ask a simple question, and I'm like, "Well someone can answer it." If they ask a hard question, I wait for an answer. So, I don't really participate in lectures. But in [Inquiry] class, I feel more comfortable talking to others because we're all individuals, and I don't feel that I'm wasting my breath because I know that [the facilitators and students] will actually listen to what I say and think about it. The interaction (…) is different.

> [Our group] just ended up talking about what we did on the weekend, and what we were going to do this weekend, and what we did last night instead of doing stuff. We got more work done when we weren't as comfortable with each other. We obviously knew each other partially from the previous class time we spent together, but we'd all been tossed here in September and none of us [was] real clear and we didn't really know each other. So, more work was done in the beginning for sure. (…) I don't know, obviously not in all group situations [would] that sort of tactic (…) work.

> You feel comfortable as you become more used to being in a group setting, as

you become more comfortable being around the people you are working with.
And as that happens, you feel more and more comfortable expressing your
thoughts.

The majority of students claim that their comfort development occurred
over a lengthy timeframe, with some students identifying that it took four or five
months to gain familiarity with Inquiry and others saying it required twelve
months or more. Over time, students are able to reflect back on their Inquiry
experience and identify with confidence what they have learned. (To learn more
about self-reflection, turn to page 83) A few examples exist in contrast to these
results; in these examples, students explain that they have never achieved a
sense of comfort. One student attributed the lack of comfort development to the
structure of Inquiry itself, explaining that Inquiry brought to light the student's
limitations as a learner. Other students attribute insecurity to what they perceive
to be a competitive atmosphere amongst BHSc students.

I felt that Inquiry was a useful course but it took me a semester to feel comfortable within that setting. I believe that this might be the case with many
other students who are new to the Inquiry process.

My general experience of Inquiry has been one of discomfort. Upon entering
the Bachelor of Health Sciences program, I was immediately confronted with
my weaknesses as a student and as a human being. Quickly, Inquiry made me
aware of my limitations as a learner. It taught me things about myself that I
didn't know before. For example, it taught me that I have a high reliance on
commercial search engines as my primary source for research: a source of information that is not very reliable.

Now, in fourth year, I can't say I have Inquiry all figured out, but through the
process, I know more about myself and how [I should] approach different
situations. I'm confident I have gained the skills to adjust to working with new
individuals and new ideas and to direct my own learning.

Personally, the competitive atmosphere in first year caused me to shy away
from the BHSc culture. I instead formed friendships with people in other faculties, because I didn't want to constantly be talking and thinking about school
and classes.

Satisfaction and Dissatisfaction

Although the Inquiry journey can be lifelong, upon the completion of a particular Inquiry project, a student can feel a level of satisfaction or dissatisfaction.
After becoming more familiar with Inquiry, most students feel their learning to
be more rewarding and effective. They are satisfied with what they have accomplished and what they have learned along the way. If students enjoy Inquiry and
believe it is more effective than traditional methods, they feel satisfied with using this self-directed approach and adamantly express how much it has positively influenced their learning. However, there are students who do not prefer

Inquiry and would rather engage in lecture-based learning formats. This dissatisfaction can have different implications on students' learning. If a student is dissatisfied with Inquiry methods, his or her learning is negatively affected using this approach, especially if he or she does not believe it is effective and appropriate.

The majority of Inquiry students identify their extreme satisfaction with Inquiry in the BHSc Program. These quotations illustrate students' satisfaction with Inquiry and give examples of a few students' dissatisfaction with Inquiry.

Satisfaction:

> I would say [I am satisfied] because I understand [Inquiry] more. I know some people don't like it, but personally I have no problem with it. (...) I actually like it. I enjoy it. I don't know if I'd [have] enjoyed it as much at the beginning of my education in university because I didn't understand it, but as I grew to understand more of what was the point, then I was able to appreciate it more.

> Every Inquiry experience I had ended up good, you know, whether or not there were small setbacks here and there. That's just a part of life learning and school, and everything in the end you pull together and it all turns out okay.

> I'm pretty satisfied, I would say, because I think my Health Science courses are the most interesting ones. I [would] so much rather be doing [Inquiry style courses] than sitting in a [non-Inquiry style] course or something, writing notes and memorizing things.

> Personally, I love Inquiry over lecture-style learning. I go to a lecture and even if I read the material before I go, it's just, I don't know, someone just blabbing at you, right? It's so easy to be turned off by the professor in many different ways whether it's the way they speak, what they talk about, whether it's of interest to you or not, and I mean the whole setting. (...) I don't think it's very comfortable or conducive to my learning. If it's really boring and if I've had a late night, I'll fall asleep, whereas if I'm doing something for Inquiry, researching, (...) it's so much more interesting. You're going and doing your own research, and learning about things by going at your own pace, and figuring out things yourself. It's not like someone telling you what you're supposed to know; you have to figure it our yourself and it's so much more involved as opposed to sitting there and kind of listening, watching the professor just blab on. So for me, Inquiry is a lot better for my understanding of a topic (...) as opposed to [learning through a] lecture. I mean, maybe we may not cover such a wide range as you would in lecture. However, I think that we don't retain [lectures] as well. I know I can remember a lot of what I learned about in second year Inquiry (...). We might not have covered everything that a class or a lecture might have covered, but we wouldn't have remembered much of anything if we had done a lecture on all that stuff.

I guess, with my experience solely in BHSc, it's been a great experience, very eye-opening. I love the Inquiry classes (...). I love that whole setting where you learn things at your own pace, learn things with friends, and colleagues or students. And I think it's a great program to sort of facilitate (...) not necessarily a newer way, but what I would consider a better manner, in which you learn new material. It's not set out [in a format where someone decides] "This is what you have to learn." You go for what you want to learn and it's an amazing program, and I've had such a great experience that way, and I've really enjoyed it because of that.

I absolutely hated Inquiry in first year, and now I want to become a peer tutor for [first year] Inquiry. I want to help others understand that it will get better, and that a course is as valuable as you make it. If you choose to stick with it, you will learn more than you ever thought possible.

Dissatisfaction:

[Inquiry] tries to separate itself from the university and granted that's probably what the people who founded the program wanted it to be (...). But I think you can only take it so far until you start to affect the students. If your [program]'s removed from the rest of the [programs], you're not getting a really good university experience. You're only associating most of the time with the same people and I had to make a conscious effort to associate with people outside of [BHSc], especially in first and second year when the majority of the people that you know are in your [program] or in your residence.

I think that Inquiry and the whole PBL experience are great. I do, however, think that trying to force so much PBL on the first years is a little much. Students should take general science courses to build a better background in the area and then apply their knowledge using the PBL process.

I think I was a little disappointed when nothing seemed to be happening to me right away, even though I was working hard at learning. My first two Inquiry projects, one for each semester of first year, were certainly valuable learning experiences, but I always felt that they never got off the ground. My group members and I never seemed to get caught up in our topics or the research. By the end of first year, I was still struggling to put together my conception of Inquiry. I had a much better idea of what it was, but I couldn't back this idea up with anything definitive from my experience. Maybe there just hadn't been enough time.

Some days, [Inquiry] seemed like a waste of time to sit around for three hours when few classmates were willing to contribute to the discussion and even fewer had any idea of what we were supposed to be discussing in the first place, [including myself]. When we turned to the facilitators or tutors for help, we just had our questions thrown right back at us [in the form of another question].

I struggled with the Inquiry course at first. I did not participate in the class discussion as much as I would have liked partly because I felt some topics which we discussed weren't very interesting. In one of my Inquiry classes in first year, someone began discussing something which many students found uninteresting and pointless, and it made me question the importance of Inquiry and why the BHSc put such an emphasis on this learning method.

When students tell me that the program is easy, it makes me ask why I am struggling so much within the program. My marks are higher in courses that I take outside the program, not in Health Science courses. Such comments have also made me question whether Inquiry style learning actually works. One significant event that I can recall is an event that occurred during the first term. The (…) students [in another faculty] were studying for a (...) mid-term, and they were struggling on certain concepts. What bothered me is that I couldn't help them because they were learning topics that were completely different from what I was learning in [a similar BHSc course]. I felt that their knowledge was more expansive than mine in the area (…). This made me question exactly what I was learning in [my Inquiry-based course] and if [the subject] was something that could be approached in a problem-based or Inquiry way. I am still left feeling unsure of what I am learning and how well I am learning.

Have you ever had an emotional experience? Do you empathize with some of the emotions described above?

3.2 Facilitators

Box 3.1
Let's Introduce the Facilitator!

You are a first year BHSc student, entering Inquiry class for the first time. The class, you have learned, is composed of a small group of students, but how the class will be run remains a mystery. You are naturally a bit anxious.

Upon entering the room, you see your classmates but to your surprise, no professor standing at the front of the room. Could he or she be late? After looking around, you finally locate your professor sitting amongst the students! Now you are curious. Why is he or she not giving a lecture but, instead, talking with the students? How is this class going to be run? And did you just hear somebody refer to your professor by his or her first name?

These questions fill your head rapidly, but the answers, you will find, come slowly as your journey through Inquiry unfolds.

Understanding the Role of a Facilitator

[10,40,95,131][91][96] Inquiry is based on the principle of self-directed learning (SDL), meaning that students play a central role in determining their own learning goals and paths. However, SDL does not mean that learning takes place without the feedback or guidance of an expert. In the Inquiry model, facilitators fulfill the role of such an expert whose purpose is to enrich the experiences of the learner.

Interestingly, in spite of their importance, the role of facilitators may not become immediately clear to students experiencing Inquiry for the first time in an academic institution. For students who have been brought up in classrooms dictated by the instructions of an authority, they may be confused by the behavior of their facilitators, which sharply contrasts with their notion of how a teacher is "supposed" to act. One student remarked:

> At first I was very frustrated with my facilitator. She told us that what we wanted to do was up to us and stood back. When we sat in silence around our table, as we often did in the first few classes, she would not jump in and start a

---

[10, 40, 95,131] Role of a facilitator! As you read this section, think of how the elusiveness of a facilitator's role fosters self-directed learning. What are the disadvantages of this style of teaching? If you are an educator, where do you fit in the spectrum of student-centred and teacher-centred teaching?

[91] You have been introduced to the concept of facilitators in the context of student development. But what is a facilitator and how do facilitators differ from professors in today's universities? Read on to find out!

[96] You have just learned about peer tutors. In this section, we will elaborate on the role of the facilitator. What do you think is the relationship between peer tutors, facilitators, and students?

conversation, but would patiently wait for us to do so. She would also answer questions by feeding the question back to us or by asking further questions. This seemed very frustrating to me.

Even after a year of experiencing Inquiry, some students still will not understand the role of facilitators. The role of a facilitator is elusive, partially because students have such high control over their own learning; the subtle but crucial guidance of a facilitator can be easily overlooked. However, a very large majority of students gradually come to feel that facilitators play an instrumental role in aiding the acquisition of skills and development of lifelong learning values. This feeling is reflected in the following quotations:

> In first year Inquiry it did not seem like the facilitators had much of a role in my own Inquiry experience. It appeared to me that I was in charge of my own learning and that I had to discover things on my own. But looking back, I realize that the facilitators have played a beneficial role in my learning. In first year Inquiry, they gave hints as to the directions one should take and things to pay close attention to. In a sense, they guided me in my own learning.

> The facilitator would (...) sort of direct the conversation to a new direction or a new focus. In that way she is a teacher, but all she's doing is she's just opening the door for us to govern ourselves and (...) what we want to get out of [the class].

> At first, I didn't understand the role of the facilitator. I was like, "Why do they never tell us anything and why do they keep bouncing questions back at us?" I was very confused. I guess that's why I didn't speak up. I was very intimidated. I understand now, because it makes you go and look for [the answers] yourself. If you look for it yourself, you're going to remember it better than if someone just tells you the answer. If you actually have to think about what you're doing, I think it makes a much deeper impression on you. At first I don't think I saw any merit in it. But slowly, very slowly, it helped.

At the core of every good facilitator is an individual who believes in the principles of Inquiry. The particular professional background of the facilitator is not as important as whether or not he or she understands the Inquiry learning process. One student remarked about one of her facilitators:

> I know she's a [medical professional] (...) so it seems like most of her background hasn't been in the [education] field. But I think she's taught this course before and she knows what's valuable and what's not. Although [with] her, she even said that her background was more memorizing the books (...). In that way she's (...) a better facilitator because she knows what we're going through and she knows kind of what we were expecting when we came into the program. (...) She made the transition herself. She went through the same steps we did.

Without a facilitator who is an Inquirer at heart, the learning of students suffers. One student explained:

> I think some [facilitators] were still a bit unsure of the whole Inquiry way of learning. (...) Not that they were bad, but [they] just didn't have the whole perspective on what Inquiry was about.

It is debatable whether or not the professional background of the facilitator is important. Some may argue that the process of learning is transferable from field to field. The facilitator's role is to teach students to become better learners and not to transfer knowledge per se. It is indeed true that for some students, the professional background of the facilitator is not very important.

> I didn't know much about my facilitator's background and maybe would have enjoyed hearing about it and what other work she was presently working on. [Yet], I felt this had no effect on my learning.

For many students, however, the professional background of the facilitator does impact student learning. Not surprisingly, students commented that some facilitators from different backgrounds tend to bring different slants on the type of information covered in class and the style of running the class; this can be an enriching but also limiting experience.

> I was aware of the facilitators' backgrounds and I do believe this influenced my learning. In first semester of first year Inquiry, [based on my facilitator's background], I knew that an emphasis would be placed on finding appropriate resources.

> Most times I was not aware of my facilitator's background. Sometimes, however, it was easier to determine than others, based solely on the course that they were teaching (e.g. teaching a vaccines course if he had background in immunology, or teaching biochemistry if her background was in biochemistry). This may have influenced my learning in that these facilitators were able to provide novel and useful sources of information in that particular field, which helped guide the group research.

> I was aware of my facilitator's background. This influenced our learning greatly because he often spent time in class focusing on skills that related to his discipline. This was both a good and a bad thing, good because he was an expert in his area, which related very well to the skills that we were currently working on in Inquiry, and bad because we probably spent a little too much time working within his area of expertise when we could have been focusing on other subject areas.

> I think [my facilitator] did introduce herself and kind of explained, "This is what I do otherwise, outside of BHSc." And I don't know if that was necessarily important for myself, but I mean, eventually it did become sort of a good thing because [her] background kind of came out later to help me out. Her (...)

expertise helped me out with (…) skills I wanted to build upon. (…) She knew her stuff. I'm sure the path she took to become [a professional in her field] did help her (…) understand the Inquiry process.

In both first and third year, I was somewhat aware of the background of my facilitator. I think that this enhanced my experience because I did not think of them as a professor anymore. It made me feel more comfortable and it gave me more of an appreciation for the opinions and suggestions. This is because I knew more of their experiences in the areas we were studying.

Interestingly, students have commented that knowing the professional background of their facilitators can affect them emotionally. Many students have stated that after they became aware of their facilitators' backgrounds, they developed a greater sense of respect and appreciation for them. Students have also been inspired by the accomplishments of their facilitators.

I'm doing [a course with a well-accomplished facilitator] and he is outstanding. He is an outstanding facilitator. He's very knowledgeable in what (…) he's working on (…). It's just that you can tell that not only is he knowledgeable, but he is passionate about it. And that's really inspiring because it makes you not want to do well [just] for a grade. It makes you want to do well because you want to (…) be that inspired.

When my facilitator introduced himself to my class, he made us aware of his background. From that very moment, I was struck with admiration towards him. The way that my facilitator behaves towards myself and my peers reflects an understanding of us. He shows us that he knows that we are going through some difficult transitions at this point in our university careers, and he always challenges us to look for ways in which we can improve our skills. My facilitator has shown me that he is well accomplished in the skills that we are working to improve through his many achievements. This has influenced my learning significantly because my facilitator has become more than a teacher to me. He has become a role model that I seek to emulate.

I knew that my facilitator was a [medical professional], but what impressed me most was how worldly she seemed; from her description of a large number of exciting experiences in different parts of the world, I realized that she was more than just intelligent in an academic sense. She was an inspiration for me to get out there and have my own "real-life" experiences in order to learn, rather than just reading about these experiences.

Facilitators can also have different takes on exactly how they are to interact with students. Each brings his or her unique personality and expertise to the class, influencing the dynamics of the classroom.

With [facilitator A], we always had end of class discussions, but with [facilitator B] we didn't really. So that was a little different. (...) I found that with [facilitator A], because we had those end-of-class discussions, I jotted down a lot of questions (...) [because she would ask], "Well, have you [kept track of your questions]?" And [facilitator B] didn't really get [focus as much on this skill], that wasn't her drive, I guess. I guess she was more (...) task-driven instead (...).

I have a feeling that for (...) second year Inquiry, (...) the facilitators (...) are more focused on the content, (...) seeing how much research you've actually done. It's not a bad thing. It's just (...) a little different [than first year].

Students view this diversity in the teaching style of facilitators as a positive. In particular, they feel that the diversity opens them to different fields of knowledge and different perspectives on learning.

The facilitators for Inquiry are (...) fantastic. As I said, I had two facilitators first year [who] approach things very differently. Their approaches may be different but they both have so much to offer to students and I was just extremely impressed with both of my facilitators.

One notable advantage of having different facilitators with different teaching styles is that it increases the likelihood that a student can be matched with someone who brings a dynamic particularly beneficial to that student. In the following example, a student comments on his experiences having two different facilitators in his Inquiry class:

Some of our presentations in Inquiry we have in front of [facilitator A], some in front of [both of our facilitators], some that were just [facilitator B]. And the ones that were going to be [facilitator A], you're like, "Oh no, he's going to come after us; he's really going to challenge us with all these strange questions." He poses strange questions all the time. (...) Which reminds me, [facilitator A] had a really big impact on me [in terms of] looking up on stuff, because he was always challenging [my statements]. I think I learned out of Inquiry that you should really have to know everything about what you are saying, and you really have to know you can't just use a term because you read it and you know it fits. You kind of have to know everything about it. (...) [Facilitator A] would always be challenging and [facilitator B] would be less challenging and (...) wanted you to work on your skills and (...) say, "You need to do this and these are some things that are helpful." (...) But I think that [facilitator B] was less effective [for me] because of that.

In the end, no matter what the style of facilitator, they have a common goal: to help students become confident Inquiry learners.

Different facilitators have different methods of teaching, but I think that all their philosophies, having students find answers for themselves, are the same. I think they have helped me realize that I can find the answer myself for whatever I am looking for. They will direct me, but they won't give me the answer. I think that's great.

The Transition into Inquiry

[91] Students entering an Inquiry-based learning environment for the first time often feel numerous frustrations and confusions. Facilitators have an important responsibility of supporting students through this difficult time by counselling them both emotionally and academically. During moments of stress, facilitators ensure students that things will get better, and that being frustrated is a part of the Inquiry process.

> [My facilitator] was effective in that she didn't allow us to get too frustrated. And you know, we hit those points where we were all frustrated and arguing... you know, we haven't done anything and I think everyone hits that point.

> The facilitators have helped a lot. They help us (...) guide the process. They don't give us a structure; they don't [tell us], "You have to answer this question today and this question today by next week." They do, however, want to know that you are progressing and that you are progressing in a proper way. Facilitators guide: they don't tell you what to do, but make sure you are on the right track. In the end, you are still to achieve a standard, although your way of doing it is your own. If there is a concern after one month (perhaps that your research question, for example, has undefined terms or that you guys are all over the place), they help us slow down and say, "Hey look, you got to take something out of your question; you have to centralize your question." (...) They really (...) guide the project a lot [and] at the same time, [they are] allowing us to do things with a little bit of flexibility. (...) Everyone's a little different, and to give everyone a structure would seem (...) very concrete, you know. So the facilitator's role is (...) just to guide us along.

Crucially, facilitators help students appreciate the values inherent in the Inquiry process. They help students understand the intrinsic values of learning, something that will help motivate them in their future endeavours both inside and outside of school (To learn more about this topic, turn to page 16). They also help students learn to trust each other, facing their vulnerabilities when revealing their opinions in groups.[79, 81]

---

[91] You are here because you would like to learn more about how facilitators aid in student development. One of the major roles of facilitators is to help students make the transition into an Inquiry learning environment. Read on to discover how!

[79, 81] In addition to the values instilled by the Inquiry process, a culture develops in the context of Inquiry between students of the Program. The style of learning encourages a tight-knit cooperation between students both within sessions and externally. Do all students welcome this open nature of Inquiry, or is the expectation of being open, honest, and close to others overwhelming? To learn how students feel about the Inquiry culture, read more on page 79. Facilitators play a crucial role, not only in instilling the values of Inquiry and its educational styling, but also in creating the culture that develops between students. To learn more about this topic, turn to page 81.

I thought the addition of facilitators and the presence of them there and [seeing] how they worked in class was really, really good. (...) Especially in first year BHSc, you really want to engrain in [the students] that (...) learning is for learning. And it's not that easy to convert (...) someone who's been engrained so long, for like 12 years, on some other system where it's just like, you know, you work, you work, you work, you get your grade, and that's that. You don't have to care about it anymore until the next time you're tested. And so I think that the presence of the facilitators and what they did was (...) really phenomenal (...) It's essential that you have a good facilitator and they make the process just so much better.

[My facilitator would] ask a question, and you know, we'd wait for someone to answer and no one would answer. There'd be such a long pause, that was at the beginning right. And eventually, everyone got to know each other a bit better and people started speaking up and it just became such an open, relaxed environment. And I believe that she really did facilitate our learning and how to open ourselves up to the group process.

[Our facilitators] did guide our conversations. Without them, if they were just background things, then most of us in class will treat marks and product as very important. Some of us still do, but it's really hard not to focus on the end product. It's something we struggle with. It's good to learn and research and stuff, but if we don't have a focus, a goal, it feels like such a waste of time. And this is a concept the facilitators are trying to introduce to us. (...) [My facilitator] is always saying, "It's the process..."

Since facilitators play an important role in the development of their students, student-teacher rapport is strong. This sense of closeness helps students develop positive feelings about their own identity as a learner, and feel comforted knowing that they can turn to their facilitators in times of need.

After the interviews [with my facilitator], I would always leave feeling better about myself than when I came in. I was able to apply what I learned from her, not only to improving my skills, but also to solving problems I was experiencing in my life. I also felt better knowing that there was someone I could turn to if anything went wrong.

I don't feel hesitant at all when approaching [my facilitators]. I don't feel like I have anything to hide when I'm talking. They're here to help me out or they're here to listen.

I really like that [I can call my facilitators by their first names], you don't see that anywhere else. That allows us to see them as people, not as some ominous facilitator. Because of the small ratio, they know our names and what we're like. The fact that they know us makes us feel better. I think that really helps. Especially, in university, our fear as high [school students] was that we would just become a number. It's really great in this program that the facilitators know who we are. It gives a sense that someone cares about us, and I think that's very important.

In this next example, a student describes how her experiences with her facilitator has eased apprehensions concerning speaking to professors in the university. Indeed, one of the main goals of facilitators is to break down hierarchical barriers between faculty (traditionally seen as inaccessible authority figures) and students. This mutual respect between students and their facilitators is a cornerstone in the Inquiry culture. (To learn more about this culture, turn to page 105).

> The facilitators have also been very beneficial, (...). Like actually being [able] to sit down [with] professors [in interviews] (...) in first term, which I know a lot of students are pretty apprehensive about doing. (...) [Speaking to] someone who has been (...) in a professional career for so many years, it can be difficult [for students] to [talk to]... and incredibly intimidating. So [the facilitators] are good (...) in that they show you the ropes so you can get a jump on talking to [professors] (...) before a lot of students [outside the program] are even thinking about talking to [professors] (...) when they need to search up [a] thesis or something like that. So if you build up relationships with professional individuals, it definitely helps your ability to communicate with them as you progress through the years. So when you're searching for an upper year project, or a thesis, you can comfortably go to [a professor's] office, knock on [his or her] door, and ask, "Do you mind helping me through this?" And that's something [that some BHSc students] may be able to do, but not other people who didn't receive that extra boost from the Inquiry process.

Their guidance does not end with the Inquiry class; students have reported that they have built strong relationships with their facilitators outside the classroom that continue for years. Facilitators have been there for some students both as a friend and as an academic counsellor. The relationship can be helpful in establishing the idea of a community of learners in BHSc.

> The other day, I saw my facilitator and she stopped to chat. (...) She introduced me to her new Inquiry class. I'd say you do develop a way better relationship [with a facilitator] than with a [regular] professor. I don't know any of my [non-Inquiry] professors by first name; that's just unheard of (...). But, I think that with Inquiry, you are presented with that possibility [of getting to know your facilitator], and it's really neat because it's like you're learning from a person, not from a professor.

> Throughout the last [year], even [after we] finished out first year Inquiry class, [my facilitator and I] kept in touch. Or if I had questions, about 3H03 class, or which class I should take, or what I should do, or references, I've gone to her, and I've asked her silly questions, and she's never judged me for anything. (...) She's always been helpful and given me good advice and it's just something that I appreciate it a lot.

> In particular, when we're with the facilitator, it seems like we're working with the person, and not just them, you know, talking to us in a downward manner.

It's almost as if they're working alongside with us and they're helping us achieve our goals. They're not there all the time (…), they're not always with you when you're doing your work, but whenever you have something pop up or you have a problem here, you can always contact them.

The role of the facilitator played an extremely important part in my experience with Inquiry. In class, she acted as a voice of reason for the worries and naivety of the class, calming our first year fears with logic and a wealth of knowledge. She also allowed us the freedom to discuss absolutely anything we wanted during class, creating a comfortable and accommodating environment. She led us through these discussions too, spurring the opinions of everyone on pertinent issues. Outside of class, she was more than a mediator of discussion, however. To me, she was more of an academic counsellor, again, calming my naive fears and insecurities, but also giving me support and reassurance of my future in whatever I do. Today, even in second year, my facilitator remains someone I can look to for support and even friendship.

Helping Students Think on their Own

[24] The main role of facilitators is different than that of teachers in traditional pedagogy. Rather than didactically transferring knowledge to students who have little input in their own learning, facilitators subtly guide students to discover things for themselves. The belief is that if students take an active role on their own learning, setting their own goals, solving problems in their own way, and arriving at their own conclusions, they will not only become better self-directed learners, but the knowledge they acquire will be more meaningful (To learn more about the advantages of self-directed learning in Inquiry, turn to page 20).

I think the role of a facilitator is to not give us the answers, but ask the right questions so that we can think of the answers for ourselves. [They help] promote the learning instead of (…) holding our hand through it. They just sort of give us hints instead of the answer. That way, you're allowed to explore and make your own mistakes instead of knowing what's already wrong. [With too much guidance], you just don't learn as much.

You get some information [from my facilitator] but instead of just answering your question, he asks you a bunch of other questions that make you think. I

---

[24] You have just looked at the IREC model. While the process of Inquiry may look simple enough, in reality, students initially find it difficult to apply these steps in solving real-life problems. Inquiry isn't something that can be learned through books or lectures, it must be experienced! Instead of being lectured about Inquiry, students are *guided* through the IREC process by facilitators. One of the major goals of Inquiry facilitators is to help students think on their own. This section explores this topic further.

think (...) you get an answer [eventually], but you actually come up with this answer yourself.

Initially, the lack of clear directions can evoke negative emotions in the students. There is also a fine balance that facilitators must strike between being overly forceful to students and making students feel abandoned. There was only one report of a facilitator dominating the class:

> My facilitator tended to dominate the selection of topics for discussion rather than allowing conversation and discussion to flow naturally. This had both its advantages and disadvantages. It allowed us to stay on topic and learn as much as we could; however, we did not have as much freedom as other Inquiry classes.

More common was the idea that some students felt their facilitators played too subtle of a role in guiding their learning; these students believed that increased instructions and more direct disclosure of motivations (i.e. clearer declaration of their roles, what they are trying to help students discover through a particular activity) from facilitators would have helped their learning.

> I think it is stronger if you come to the conclusion on your own. But I think you also at risk of not coming to the conclusion at all. (...) And they won't tell you how they are trying to teach (...). They want you to figure that out on your own. But, then again, I would say that some validation is good. Like, what we did in the standardized patient interview (...) what's the point of that? We were given very, very little information. Go to it. How do we prepare? What are we looking for? What are we trying to get out of it? (...) Maybe we can maximize what we are trying to learn from it if we knew what we could be getting from it. So that's the [concern] I have, that their questions are always [coming] from left field. It's cause I always feel like they are trying to hint at something, but they will never tell us.

> I wish my facilitators would have been a little bit more helpful in first year than just answering my questions with a question. Given that first year is overwhelming as it is, I believe that my facilitators could have been a bit more helpful.

> In [second year] Inquiry, you don't really have [a TA to guide you]. You [just] have your facilitator who you meet with (...) once every two weeks. (...) It might have been more helpful to have someone kind of guide you along a little bit more, considering that [you are studying] (...) a topic (...) that's completely new.

Perhaps, for the reason that facilitators can sometimes withhold instructions too much from students, some students will continue to feel that their facilitators did not enhance their learning. The most extreme case of dissatisfaction about facilitators came from one student who remarked: "I didn't enjoy the facilitator position in general because I found it kind of useless." However, this student did go on to discuss some positive experiences he had with one particular facilitator. Interestingly, many students who questioned the benefit of facilitators reported that they received help from their peer tutors, illustrating that there are multiple levels of student support in the Inquiry environment (To learn more about peer tutors, turn to page 126).

> My facilitator, surprisingly, did not play a great role in my experience. As I mentioned earlier, we had two different facilitators for each semester, so I did not get to know either of them very well. Also, I got the most out of Inquiry from the two group projects that I did, and my facilitators barely had a role in it.

> Unfortunately, I don't think my facilitators had much of a role [in my learning]. I found that I learned off my peers more. Although I did learn some helpful tips and what the Inquiry process was about, I learned how to apply the process through my peers.

When facilitators strike that "right" balance in being instructive and influential, yet still allow students to direct their own learning, students report very good experiences with the learning process. Students have particularly emphasized value in experiences where facilitators helped them learn a clearly defined skill. Students have also expressed heightened motivation when they felt they were challenged by the facilitators to improve.

> I think there was one Inquiry class where our facilitator sort of set out the guidelines. We went through a month where we were all confused and we didn't know what work to do. And after a month, we had a class where the facilitator said, "You should keep a learning portfolio and you should..." So we had a little bit of structure. And then I just started keeping this journal type thing. And initially it was like, this portfolio, it is for marks. And then halfway through, I just decided to read over what I had written before and I realized there was a general transition [period] where I learned new things. And the stuff I was recording was genuine (...). And I saw some value in it. And when I had my first interview my facilitator, [she] said that [I] did learn new things and that sort of built up my confidence. And then I guess that was the transition point. My focus wasn't just marks. It was learning and getting out of it whatever I can.

> In my experience of Inquiry, my facilitator has played the role of presenting challenges to me so that I can use them as opportunities to improve my skills. For example, my facilitator took us to the Clinical [Skills] Learning Centre so that we could interview standardized patients. This challenged me to improve my communication skills. It also revealed to me that there is more to communication than one would assume. Communication requires us to listen and connect with the people in order to understand the message. It is not about simply exchanging dialogue. It is about sharing an experience. This is something that cannot be learned through reading a textbook. Also, my Inquiry fa-

cilitator has also played the role of showing me that I should always look for ways that I can improve when I am unsuccessful at performing a task.

My first year facilitator played a huge role in my experience of Inquiry. She was very blunt and to-the-point, and quickly taught us that no matter what we were taught in high school, or what we had come to think of ourselves, we needed to redefine those notions. No one escaped her criticism, and I loved that about her.

[I feel my facilitator] does a very good job in facilitating our learning. (…) It's a good balance between her telling us this is what you have to do and at the same time, she doesn't tell us, this is what you have to do. However, she directs us and sort of helps us think on our own, and by asking us questions. (…) If it's more of a goal-oriented, more personable goal, and we want to ask her about that, then she's a very helpful resource because it's good to [have] somebody (…) who knows, who's been facilitating for a while, she will help people think. And it's hard for… like for Inquiry, we were told to focus on a couple of goals, a few personal weaknesses that we feel we have. So it's sometimes hard for many people to realize their weaknesses and how they should go about working on them and why they think something is a weakness. So it helps to have the facilitator asking us questions and sort of [force] us to think about things critically.

Importantly, however, what is the right balance for one student may not be for another. While some students are uncomfortable with the lack of clear directions from some facilitators, others thrive with this ambiguity. The following quotations show that some students prefer that facilitators remain ambiguous and elusive with instructions, so that they are encouraged to think on their own:

[My facilitators] seemed to not be an influencing force rather than overseers with seemingly hidden agendas. This made us a lot more self-reliant very quickly, although it added to the confusion, and convinced us to come up with our own agendas, expectations, and products for the research we were doing.

Facilitators weren't there to give you the answers; they were there to help you and guide you (…) so that you came up [with answers for] yourself. It was frustrating at first but once you realize that's what their role is, they're very helpful. They ask you questions. I remember we asked [my facilitator] a question and he'd ask a question right back: "What do you think"? And [we thought] just answer! But it made us think of what we were actually asking (…) It was very frustrating for the first year or first few months at least, but then you realize that was their goal and they really ask these probing questions. They make you think…

[My facilitator] was very quiet at times, and you were never [quite sure]. (…) Just the fact that she wasn't saying anything made you more sort of self-critical. (…) She was just standing there and she would smile at you and you wouldn't know what you were doing, if it was right or if it was wrong. But I think that that's the entire point, that you don't know if you're right or if you're wrong, and that's the point is to find out. And (...) there is no right or wrong. Like you just go, and whatever you find out in the end that's where you got.

Hence, a particular challenge faced by facilitators is gauging the emotional status of each individual student.

Final thoughts

As our research suggests, facilitators have a critical role in the learning of students. The difficulty faced by facilitators is that they are constantly trying to strike a fine balance in terms of their involvement in students' learning process. Facilitators should be encouraged to impart into the learning experience their own personal and professional identity. Doing so helps students feel closer to the facilitator and feel inspired by the achievements of the facilitator. In the end, the performance of the facilitator can have an impact on how students experience Inquiry. An effective facilitator will help ease the student transition into the Inquiry environment. Ideally, a facilitator will guide students to become effective Inquirers; unlike teachers in the traditional sense, facilitators transfer not necessarily a set of knowledge, but rather a set of values and skills to students. To achieve this goal, above all, facilitators must be effective Inquirers themselves. In the end, what is a facilitator? We feel that the following quotation gives a comprehensive summary:

> The role of the facilitator played an extremely important part in my experience with Inquiry. In class she acted as a voice of reason for the worries and naivety of the class, calming our first year fears with logic and wealth of knowledge. She also allowed us the freedom to discuss absolutely anything we wanted during class, creating a comfortable and accommodating environment. She led us through these discussions too, spurring the opinions of everyone on pertinent issues. Outside of class, she was more than a mediator of discussion however. To me, she was more of an academic counsellor, again, calming my naïve fears and insecurities, but also giving me support and insecurities, but also giving me support and reassurance of my future in whatever I do. Today, (...) my facilitator remains someone I can look to for support and even friendship.

3.3 Skill Development

Benefits of the Inquiry Method
    [26][73] Experiencing Inquiry for the first time can be a frustrating and ardu-

---

[26] You have just seen the BHSc skill set. The idea of focusing on skills rather than content may be an idea that is foreign to you. This section will elaborate on the rationale behind a skill-based curriculum, expand on some of the skills, and explore how student development has been impacted. Read on!
[73] Students can internalize their Inquiry experience in many ways. In this section, we will explore the Inquiry journey under the paradigm of skill development.

ous process. At first, students who are going through it might be tempted to return to the tried-and-true didactic approach to learning, especially if they feel like they're going around in circles (a common occurrence in the early stages of the Inquiry process). Many questions arise in the minds of confused and doubtful students when they are subjected to Inquiry: Is it really worth it? Why do I feel like I haven't made any progress so far? What am I going to learn from Inquiry that I wouldn't have learned otherwise?

It may take students a long time to recognize the value of the Inquiry process, sometimes a semester, sometimes a year, sometimes even longer. Eventually, the benefits of Inquiry become clear, and students realize that they have developed a number of skills that they may not have gained in a didactic education environment. A quotation from a student interview illustrates this point:

> I don't think [my skill development has] been like an all of a sudden kind of thing! I think it's more like, now when I look back, I realize that I have changed and that I have learned different skills as opposed to knowing it [at the time of taking the class]. I don't think I knew it then. I don't think at that moment, when I learned something, I said, "Oh I have learned this." I don't think I saw the value of what I had learned until later on.

Furthermore, many students recognize that the skills they acquired in Inquiry are transferable to other situations in school, at work and almost every other aspect of their lives.

> Well I think that Inquiry is more useful for the future. Skills that you'll learn from Inquiry you can apply, whether you keep going on in school, or if in the workplace, or just in regular daily life. Whereas in other courses, you're just learning the material, or just understanding it, but you might not need to apply it later on, in the future.

> I have found that some of the knowledge [learned in university] can also be transferred [to future situations], but I won't remember it, right? So I think [knowledge] is not the best thing to concentrate on in university. I think the skill development is the way to go, because it will stay with you, hopefully for a longer time and you can use that in the future.

Some of the skills that students can develop and improve on through the Inquiry process include:
1. Research and critical thinking;
2. Time management;
3. Reflection and feedback;
4. Communication and social/interpersonal skills; and
5. Learning/working in a group

In this section of the book, we will investigate the first four areas, focusing on the improvements that BHSc students have made throughout their Inquiry experience.

Research Skills

In the traditional didactic approach to teaching, professors instruct students about what information they need to learn. Typically, the information students are expected to know comes from lecture notes and assigned textbook readings, among few other sources. They are expected to learn this information and demonstrate their mastery of the subject area through tests, assignments, and other forms of evaluation. When students brought up under the didactic approach experience Inquiry for the first time, they tend to assume that their facilitators are going to give them instructions in the way that a traditional professor would. Much to their dismay, an Inquiry facilitator leaves it up to the students to select the topics that they want to focus on, and expects them to find the sources of information they need in order to answer their own questions. Depending on the situation, students may receive minimal guidance, or at times, no instructions at all. This lack of direction makes it necessary for students to develop their own research process, asking and refining questions, determining which sources of information will answer their questions, critically evaluating those information sources, and synthesizing their results to come up with an answer or new questions. All of these skills acquired in the research process are emphasized in the BHSc Inquiry curriculum. Many students in the program have attested to the fact that Inquiry courses have significantly improved their research skills, as shown in the quotations below:

> For me, Inquiry is about self-directed learning, to go out there on your own without the aid of a course or any type of structure. So I equate it to being in the real work force. It's like you have to achieve a goal, without a lot of other people holding your hand. So I found it really useful in that sense, and it wasn't something I really thought about in first year. Inquiry for me seemed very research oriented. I'd get a topic, I'd research it out, then go about setting up questions to further my research and stuff like that, only to produce the technical "final product" for the person who asked me the question to begin with. And I didn't really make the connection to the workforce, until I was working in the summer and I realized that a lot of the jobs that people are looking for, the high quality jobs, use the same skills, but are attempting to answer different questions.

> [Inquiry] makes you learn a different way, like, [it] encourages asking questions and things like that more than just studying from a textbook; [Inquiry requires that] you to use more resources (...). I can learn a lot more myself now, like if I have a question, I know where to find answers and things like that. I know how to use resources now. I know how to approach things, not just from one path. However I want to do it, I feel like I'm capable, like I have the skills. I have the tools to be able to do things my way, or how I want to do it.

> Based on first year, my understanding was that Inquiry was to (...) develop a question of interest and, in a group, pursue it, research it. [In] second year, I

guess that was kind of changed a bit in that we were given this small amino acid sequence and [were] expected to figure it out from there. So I guess I'd say Inquiry is (...) more or less, establishing the problem at hand, understand[ing] what the question is, and then by looking at those points, researching [and] asking questions. Hopefully, you don't have to find the answer necessarily to the question, but gain a better understanding of the question. Usually you do that through research (...) through journals, books, newspapers, any sort of source of information.

Students often find that the research skills they gained in Inquiry are transferable to future academic situations. One student's testimonial below shows how they applied their research skills in a second-year problem-based learning course:

So you learn throughout by applying (...). For example, just a brief overview of what we did: In first term, we (...) built our research skills and learned how to use the different research programs. And in second year, we got to apply the skills we learned about research to an actual problem, so we actually learned how to learn more about [our selected topic]. So we learned how to research (...) [the topic]. So now the thing is, by learning how to research, we're able to apply it to any topic. So Inquiry actually helps you learn. (...) I don't want to say the right way to learn because there are many ways to learn, but a useful way to learn.

One skill that is closely tied to the research process emphasized in Inquiry is critical thinking. The amount of information available to university students, through sources such as books, newspaper articles, scholarly journals and web pages, can be overwhelming. The reality is that, in the academic world, these sources of information are not considered equally credible. The need to appraise credibility is especially important in cases when conflicting viewpoints or facts are presented by different sources.

Take a moment and think of an example where you saw something in the news or read something that turned out to be a hoax later on. How did this affect you? What did you learn from the experience?

Inquiry emphasizes this idea to students, teaching them not only how to find sources of information but also how to analyze them critically and determine how reliable they are. For example, if Inquiry students read a newspaper article that describes the results of a research study, they are encouraged to locate and use the original study as their primary source of information, rather than the newspaper article (in which the journalist may have misinterpreted or oversimplified the findings of the original study). Many of the students that were interviewed attested to the fact that Inquiry has improved their critical thinking skills:

> Even now, I'm doing my thesis project and I can read some published articles and they talk about other studies, and they, for example, will say, "25 percent of patients did this and that." But when I actually go to the original article, I find that this information is not necessarily true. (...) I wouldn't have done that before, [going to the original article]. I have changed a lot. I acquired a lot of skills that make me question and go on to research this and that.

> Another part of [the research process] is to evaluate the source of information that you are using, be mindful of "Okay, this is a newspaper clipping, I don't know how reliable it is." Whereas, you know, you can go to a journal database and be like, "Okay, this has been peer evaluated; it has, you know, greater trust (...) [and] truthfulness.

Some students have even transferred this skill of appraisal to their everyday lives, critically analyzing information that they once would have accepted as fact without questions. Here is a quotation from a student who now applies critical thinking to family life:

> People tell me information, and before I just [...] took it as a given. Now, I think more critically about this information and that helps me a lot with my professional development and daily life. I can give you an example. Before I got into [Inquiry], I used to take everything my mom tells me as a given. She's actually a physician; she always used to tell me do this and do that and you wont get sick. But now after I've taken these courses, I start questioning her. I started asking her for evidence. But that was cool, I found. This is one of my examples where you can actually use [Inquiry] in your daily life.

As you can see, several students in the BHSc Program have found that the Inquiry process has ameliorated their research and their critical thinking skills, skills that they will be able to apply in future academic experiences.

Time Management

As you may have learned in earlier sections, Inquiry is a process that is largely guided by the students experiencing it, and the facilitator takes a relatively passive role in this educational approach.

Students are responsible not only for determining their own areas of interest in their Inquiry process, but also for devising a plan to answer the questions that they come up with in those areas.

Part of this planning involves coming up with a timeline for the Inquiry process, from the earlier stages of defining a question and identifying useful resources to the later stages of synthesizing information and coming up with an answer to the original question.

Of course, flexibility in personal timelines is limited by the structure of university, as students must be evaluated at the end of each term. Since there is little intervention from the facilitator throughout the Inquiry process, it is the students' responsibility to make sure that they adhere to their timeline so that they can complete their project before their evaluation.

Evaluations can take many forms, such as a presentation, an essay, or progress meetings with a facilitator.

Many students in the BHSc Program have found that Inquiry has improved their time management. The following are some testimonies that BHSc students have given with respect to the time management skills they have gained through Inquiry:

One of the first skills [I learned] is time management. That is the big one; I have to be able to balance everything. So it's helping me balance my dance schedule, my social life, and my academic life. And it's hard to get everything conglomerated.

I know last year I worked heavily on my time management (...). And this is one skill that is applicable not only during the school year [but] in the summer as well. I know during this past summer [...], I [went] into my days now thinking, "Okay, what do I want to do before, what do I want to do by this time, what do I want to do before I go to bed."

So in the beginning [of our project], we got a lot of class time to work on it. The biggest thing we did at the beginning was [that] we drew out [an] outline for our presentation: so, what we wanted to cover, where we think we could find information. (...) So we could see down the road where we wanted to be. We also drew out a little bit of a timeline (...) [by deciding] when we wanted the presentation to be almost finished, so we could run over it a few times before we actually had to present to the class. And for us, as a group we decided, it would probably work better if we broke up the sections so that people could spend individual time working on the different sections. So I think that was definitely a huge benefit. Not trying to do it all as a group. Because I think if we tried to do it all as a group, it wouldn't be finished on time.

Reflection and self- / peer- evaluation
[26] Unlike traditional methods of education (such as lecture-based teaching), Inquiry emphasizes learning that is guided by the student. In Inquiry-based learning, students come up with their own questions and devise and implement a plan of action to find answers to those questions. In a process like this, where students direct their own learning (be it individually or in a group) with little intervention from the facilitator, it becomes essential for students to monitor

---

[26] As you read this section, try to come up with advantages and disadvantages of self and peer-evaluation compared to traditional evaluation methods? What are the inherent ideologies behind each method?

their own progress along the way to make sure that they stay on track. Throughout the Inquiry process, students occasionally need to pause and reflect on the progress they've made so far, determining which of their methods have been effective and which ones have not.[37] Many of the students who were interviewed commented on the importance of self-reflection in Inquiry:

> [Inquiry is] learning without even knowing you're learning. You know, you are picking things up and you don't really realize it. It's kind of cool. Which is why I guess self-evaluation is so important. Otherwise, you wouldn't realize how far you've come.

Think about a time in your life where you had to evaluate your strengths and weaknesses. Were you able to identify your weaknesses and work to improve them? Was the process beneficial?

Through the process of self-evaluation, students can identify the areas that they excel in and the areas where they need improvement. They can then focus on improving in their areas of weakness and refine the approaches they took in the past to work more efficiently in future endeavours.

> [Inquiry has] given me a lot of chance for self-reflection, to think about what my strengths are, and what my weaknesses are, and how I can go about changing them.

> [Through] all the reflections that we've had to do, I've been able to get better at my strengths and look at improving my weaknesses.

> I am doing a lot better this term already, because last term, towards the end, (…) I really looked at what I needed to do. I did self-evaluation, (…) figuring what I did wrong this term and what I needed to change. And that's what I have been doing, you know. I have been trying to keep up and I have been doing pretty [well].

Students can take a similar evaluative approach when working in groups, exchanging feedback with other group members. Some stu-

---

[37] Self and peer reflections are crucial in the Inquiry process, particularly to explore the diverse range of feelings experienced during Inquiry. To learn more about these feelings, turn to page 37.

dents have expressed that they value peer feedback more than self-evaluation, since it is difficult to self-evaluate in an honest and objective way:

> I think [self-evaluation] is valuable, but it may not be accurate. You are evaluating yourself. Like I can say, "Oh, I've changed." But sometimes it's your peers or your group members that help you realize that as well, when they tell you [that] maybe you should [do something differently]. It kind of helps you adjust and realize that maybe you're not necessarily doing things wrong, but that there are different ways of doing things.

Many students in the BHSc Program have said that giving and receiving feedback from peers has been beneficial to their learning process. The quotations below highlight some of the things that students expressed about feedback skills:

> One of the biggest things that [are] focused on [in] first/second year Inquiry is giving and receiving feedback to your peers and critically evaluating your own performance. And I feel that in this class especially, it's important to know how to properly give feedback to somebody, and at the same time, it's important to be able to hear feedback. Sometimes a lot of people have a difficult time in listening to critical evaluation, but realistically, it's for your own good. So what I really like about our first/second year Inquiry (…) is [how we're] consistently giving and receiving feedback to your peers. In [my third year Inquiry class], it is a necessity to be able to say to somebody, "Listen, I don't think that question was appropriate; maybe you could have said it like this." And similarly, it is important to have somebody to tell you that.

> In the midst of all our Inquiry projects, we have been given tons of time [and] we have been given evaluations. [An evaluation] (…) gives me an opportunity to sit down and reflect. And in this reflection, you really do think about everything that has gone on, and every (…) little skill that you have developed, regardless of how big or small it is.

> The value of reflection is another thing that is good. One of the prototypical [Inquiry skills] is getting and receiving feedback. You don't really get [that] elsewhere [in non-BHSc courses], usually.

One student in particular shared a story that shows the value of receiving honest feedback from peers:

> For my interview, the midterm one that's in December, I asked all my group members in [all of my health science classes] (...) for feedback on me: on how I communicate, how I research, how I lead, whatever, all that stuff. And it was revealing because I got all this information about [how I] deliver criticism in a way that seems pretty harsh. (…) I have my own experiences correlated with [their feedback] because I realize that a lot of the times, people end up having this sort of hostile feeling towards me, and I don't really feel that I've de-

served it, because I don't feel hostile towards them. It's just the way I [communicated] the criticism.

In this case, the feedback that the student received from his peers brought attention to a problem that he was not previously aware of. Without that feedback, he would not have recognized this shortcoming, nor would he have been able to work on it in the future.

In summary, students in the BHSc Program have found that Inquiry courses have improved their group- and self-evaluation skills, enabling them to identify and improve upon their weaknesses.

Communication and Social / Interpersonal Skills

Although Inquiry is a process that can be done individually, there are many instances, particularly in the BHSc Program, where group learning is utilized. On one hand, completing an Inquiry project with a group of people increases the potential amount of work that can be done in the time allotted; on the other hand, many complexities can arise because individuals in a group have conflicting opinions about what they should do and how they should do it. Often, there will be a group in which some members who are less extraverted hesitate to voice their opinions, while other members are more assertive and make decisions for the entire group. Because Inquiry emphasizes the process of self- and group-evaluation, individuals that are normally shy in a group environment are encouraged to share their opinions about their group's progress and any possible problems that they perceive. Many students in the BHSc Program have found that Inquiry has improved their ability to communicate in a group setting by encouraging them to share their opinion with others:

> I would say that my greatest Inquiry achievement would be the fact that being put into a group, I've been able to improve my communication among the group, being able to speak up in situations where I normally wouldn't. Being able to express my views and being able to express my opinions and thoughts whenever they contribute.

> I feel a little more comfortable talking to people, being willing to email a person, or being willing to call a person, even if [I'm] requesting information, not being shy to do sessions such as [this interview]. I don't know. I think beforehand, I may [have been] a little intimidated by something like this [interview], whereas now, I'm like "Hey, this is a cool experience to talk to someone about this stuff."

Some students have also expressed the fact that these group communication skills will be applicable to future situations in their lives:

> It makes you a lot more ready to interact out in society with people. I mean, if you think about it, there are a very few professions, I can't even think of one off the top of my head, where you're not going to be working with anyone.

(...) Every profession, no matter what you do, there's going to be some sort of interaction, whether it be with a customer, a client, or a co-worker, or your boss, or your administrator. It's important to be able to have those people skills, and I think that the Inquiry program (...) really gives you the opportunity to build those skills. So when you go out to the workforce, you're not starting out from scratch. You're not starting as someone who's had their nose in their books for five years.

Coming to university, yes, you are trying to learn the knowledge, the facts. But also, there's an experience that you won't get inside the work world. You won't necessarily be in school again, learning to socialize. It's something that you're going to need for the rest of your life: how to deal with people. After you leave, you may not need those facts. No one is ever going to ask you to list, I don't know, all the body parts randomly. But, you are still going to have to learn how to interact with people. You'll work with many different types of people [in groups]. You're going to want to know how to handle yourself in those situations.

Another aspect of Inquiry in the BHSc Program that enables students to work on their communication skills is access to a clinical skills lab, where they can take part in simulated interviews with medical patients. These interviews require students to have a conversation with someone whom they've never met and build a rapport with the simulated patient. Many students in the program have found that these exercises were beneficial, and will prepare them for their professional career in the future:

What I like the most about [the simulated interviews] is that you could do an interview, and you could watch other people from behind a mirror screen. In addition to that, all of our things are videotaped and so we can actually go back and review the tape and say, "This is what I was thinking at this moment, and this is why I asked that question." And what I really like about it so far, I think we've only been in [the course] for three weeks, is that we've been able to review tapes and pinpoint moments when we could have showed more empathy or [asked] open-ended questions rather than a closed-ended question. In three weeks, it has already really improved my communication skills in terms of interviewing. So yeah, it's phenomenal.

[Simulated patient interviews] gave me a chance to talk to patients in the exact setting as we are sitting in right now. And to structure the interview appropriately so that you can [be prepared] for professional schools later on; so you will be able to sit down, and converse with patients; so they respect you as a clinician and you get the information that you need; so you can make proper decisions and diagnosis, and uphold that patient-provider relationship.

Drawbacks of the Inquiry Method
While the Inquiry method does have its benefits in terms of skill development, there are some students who thought that this style of learning does have certain drawbacks. In particular, many students feel that Inquiry courses focus

too much on the development of particular skills and not enough on providing the background relevant to the subject they are studying. Some of them felt that this will put them at a disadvantage in future situations, when they will not have adequate scientific background in spite of the skills that Inquiry has helped them to develop (e.g. group work and time management). The quotations below show some students' thoughts on the disadvantages of Inquiry-based learning:

> I think [the lack of background knowledge is] a huge flaw. Because for [one of our classes], I had not wanted to take the [Inquiry-based version of the] course because I didn't think it would cover the basics that you would need if you wanted to do something in research, which I'm considering. So when I went into the class and wanted to decide, everyone was talking about how great it will be to work closely with the professor and to do Inquiry again. Since I learned so much from the first semester Inquiry course, I thought I might be making the wrong decision. So I switched into the Inquiry course and I constantly, because my housemates were in the [non-Inquiry version of the course], I would keep track [of] what they were doing, and what I was doing. I always thought that I was behind them, and [that] I didn't know as much as them, and I didn't get that breadth that I should have. And when I was working in particular with my [Inquiry] group, we were working on [our selected topic] and we all had such different views that we got nowhere for the first month. We had agreed at the time to basically go our own way, and then we'd decide. But we never ended up [agreeing] because we had such strong people working together, and we all had such strong opinions of what the project should be that it didn't work. For me, like I said before, I wanted to know the basics (...). And everyone else was like, no, it's all about the process, but that's not my goal.

> Inquiry works great for certain things but when you need a foundation (...), you need structure. And that may be completely different from what Inquiry is, but I think it's so important to have that foundation. We were all so lost in our [class, because instructors] were trying to promote this Inquiry style method with [the] 'What do you think?' [mentality]. We were left with sort of no answers (...) because we had many groups, and so much to do, and summaries due every week. And there was so much to read, and we wanted to include different journals and textbooks and sources. [The basic] questions (...), for me at least, they were left behind.

> We discussed this many times. In Inquiry, I think, there should be a balance. I don't think you should [go] straight into Inquiry without background knowledge.

> [One drawback of Inquiry is that] you don't know if you've covered all the [important] material. (...) [In] Inquiry, I don't know if I learned the stuff that I was "supposed" to learn.

3.4 Personal Growth

The clouds overhead suffuse the night sky like a mysterious haze. Below is your house, a small spark under the shadow of a world yet to be explored. You sit in front of your fireplace, inside which a great fire captures your eyes and your imagination. Inside your head, a similar fire rages, the fire of conflicting thoughts and contending feelings. You have yet to understand why you are feeling this way. You have yet to place your thoughts in logical order, and thus make sense of the world around you. Something intrinsically doesn't make sense, a new experience challenges the old order, and your mind grasps desperately for new overarching principles to help put the fire at ease. But it is no use. The fire rages on. You are resolute, however, and you will not give up. Suddenly, there is something about the night that you find strangely seductive. You are hesitant about leaving the comfort of your warm fireplace, but the darkness beckons you. You obey. Slowly, you make your way out into the unknown. You close your eyes and the clouds begin to encircle you. They spin faster and faster, fanning the flames of your fire. Faster and faster they spin until your flames reach their pinnacle. Faster and faster until your every foundation is about to set ablaze, leaving nothing left but the all-encompassing darkness of your mind. And then, just when you feel that the combustion will consume your entire being, the fire stops. Something clicks. Within seconds the flames fade, leaving instead hot cinders of insight. The conflicting thoughts are synthesized into a unified whole. The contending feelings harmonize. Suddenly, everything makes sense again. What's more, everything makes more sense.
Congratulations. You've just had an epiphany.

From your experiences, describe the last time you feel you had an epiphany. Does the description above accurately describe how you felt?

Personal Development: Four Stories from Inquiry Students

[91] Obviously, not all instances of personal development are as dramatic as the illustration given above, and likewise, not all instances of personal development take the form of abrupt and enlightening epiphanies. Artists and poets have for centuries idealized that "eureka" moment, but in reality, personal development occurs in many different forms. It may be as subtle as it is dramatic. It may take years to occur, or it may take days. It may be driven from within, or it may be sparked by some external stimulus.

Inquiry students capture this broad range of experiences. There are those who, through inspiration from others, find their true calling. There are others who, through their own reflections, shift their worldviews and gain a greater insight into life. There are still others who believe that at the bottom of personal development and life-long learning is the principle of being open to new ideas. As one Inquiry student remarks:

> I don't think that life-long learning necessarily means that you're always learning. I just think it's always about opening your eyes and opening your beliefs, and your security, and your safe hold on what is right. [It is also about] listening to other people, and valuing other people, and never saying, "Okay, this is what I believe, and it's never going to change." You always have to be open to change, open to the possibility that someone's going to come along and shake what you've believed for the past 20 years.

Moreover, not only does personal development encompass a wide range of experiences, it is also notoriously difficult to define. At the heart of this process, nevertheless, is the gaining of greater insight about oneself, of others, and of the world. One Inquiry student defines it as "pursuing personal goals and pushing oneself to the limit to see what one can achieve." Another defines it as "the process of self-discovery and a way of life whereby one uses every opportunity to learn and develop both personally and professionally." [60, 37]

For some students, personal development may involve the acquisition of new skills; for one student it is the process of "learning new skill sets, such as how to ask meaningful questions and how to go about navigating through end-

---

[91] Group work and collaboration shapes student experiences in profound ways. This section follows the lives of four BHSc students as they grow during their undergraduate experience. As you are reading, try to think of how some of these changes may be influenced by the process of collaboration.

[60, 37] Personal growth is a unique process for each individual student. For some students, the most important part of this process is the acquisition and development of new skills. Other students' personal growth may be on more of an emotional level; for example, through the process of Inquiry they may become more confident and comfortable sharing their ideas with others. To learn about students growing through their skill development, go to section 3.3, "Skill Development", on page 60. To explore students' emotional growth, go to section 3.1, "Emotions", on page 37.

less amounts of information to answer these questions" For other students, personal development means embracing new ideas and feeling confident that those ideas can be put into practice. As one Inquiry student attests:

> [Inquiry] made me, in a sense, more driven to do what I want to do. But it has also helped me become more interested in research, and I've actually gone out to find different areas to do more research in. All and all, it has motivated me to consistently improve the way that I go about learning because [I've] been taught reflections, self-evaluations, group evaluations, and going about things in unique manners. So that has allowed me to continue to see the value in the process of the Inquiry program and to find unique ways to apply it to my daily life. So as a student, I can complete my tasks, stay on time, and continue working towards who I wish to be: someone who can be of benefit to society and the healthcare field. So it has affirmed rather than dispelled my future aspirations as a doctor. Knowing what I do now, I know what I can do can benefit others, because I've used it in so many different contexts, and [I] can apply it towards a career of that nature.

Below are the stories of four very special Inquiry students who, like the students quoted above, have struggled and triumphed through the process of personal development. Some of these students are now reflecting back on what they have learned, while others are still in the midst of their development and are unsure of where they are headed. These four stories were chosen not only because they exemplify different aspects of the personal development journey, but also because they are vivid, detailed, and honest portrayals. These stories are told from the students' perspectives. Names and identifying features, however, have been changed to protect the individual student's identity

Monica: Third year, female student

When I was in high school I was a perfectionist. I was always concerned about marks, and I was very competitive. I wanted to be the best at everything, and I was very stubborn. Because of this, I would often get into conflicts with people, but I was still determined to prove to others that I was right. Later on when I came into the BHSc Program, things changed. Things have evolved over the past few years, and they are continuing to change. I don't think there ever was one real turning point when I realized that perfectionism wasn't the way to go. You don't wake up one minute and realize, "Oh that doesn't matter to me anymore." For me, it was always a journey. Experiences build onto other experiences, until one day you realize that what used to bother you doesn't matter anymore.

But there were specific incidents that helped me with my progression. One of the most important was first-year Inquiry because it was in this class that I met Alice. I shared the same Inquiry group with Alice, and I had to work with her for the entire year. The experience was a difficult one because she had values that totally conflicted with mine. You see, at the time I was beginning to realize that I was a perfectionist, and I was trying to change my values and my priorities. I was trying to switch my focus from "school is everything" to "there's more to life than school." However, Alice was still very driven and competitive, very much like how I was in high school. I saw in her something I was trying to move away from, and because of this, it was very difficult to deal with her. Frankly, I didn't know how to accept her values anymore, and as a result, I really did not like her.

But one day everything changed, and my first year facilitator had a lot to do with that. My facilitator was very good at getting to know me in a way that I had not anticipated. I felt like by the end of the course, my facilitator knew me more than anyone else at the university and I felt that she understood where I was coming from. She knew more about what I had taken from my experiences and my journey than I think I even did.

Throughout the year she told me, simply put, that things would be okay. She also told me to be more open and to learn from other people, to be open to people and what they have to say. I learned from her that fighting with people was not going to change the way they thought, but that setting an example through action was the best way to demonstrate my values.

After talking with my facilitator, I realized that Alice was more than just an embodiment of those values I had tried dearly to move away from. She was a person too, and there was more to Alice than my conception of her. She was someone whom I could learn from, and she was someone could learn from me. I realized also that if I were more accepting of her, maybe she too would become more accepting of me. If I wanted to help Alice realize that there was more to life than school, arguing with her and clashing with her all the time was not going to work. I could never demonstrate the merit of my values through conflict. But by being open-minded with Alice, I could share with her my experiences and understand her experiences as well.

So it was in First Year Inquiry where I was forced to deal with people like Alice. The class gave me the opportunity to interact with other people and to learn that being different was no excuse for not interacting and getting along with others. As a result, a lot of my current perspective on life was formed at the end of first year.

Nowadays, I have a fairly solid perspective on life. It's basically that, I guess it has sort of a religious aspect to it, as a person I want to strive to be closer to God. That's where everything stems from. By being close-minded, not accepting, and judgmental pulls me away from being a better person. So when I encounter people with different opinions or when there's conflict, I need to look at the situation and realize that I have no need to get angry or continue the argument. Instead, I need to ask myself: Where are they coming from? What experiences do these other people have that I may not be aware of? And what experiences don't they have that may be promoting them to think and act in a certain way? So when dealing with other people, I have to keep in mind that they've gone through a different set of life experiences, struggles, challenges and triumphs. That's why every day I need to empathize with other people, to look at the world from their perspective, and to learn from others what I can.

Jessica: First year, female student

One of my biggest problems is communicating with other people. In the past, I had no idea that I had this problem, and it was only when we started talking about effective communication in first year Inquiry that I started to realize how important communication skills were. What really helped me identify this problem was the peer feedback I received as part of the Inquiry process. In preparation for my midterm Inquiry interview with my facilitator, I asked all my group members in my Inquiry class and my peer tutors to give me feedback. I asked them to comment on how well I communicated, how well I researched, how well I led, and stuff like that. The feedback was very revealing because I got a lot of comments that really surprised me. For example, one of my peers stated that I delivered criticism in a way that seemed pretty harsh. This theme continued in the other feedback that I received as well.

It was then that I put two and two together. I started to recall some of my personal experiences, and I could remember that a lot of the times, my peers displayed a certain amount of hostility towards me. Until then, I didn't really know why. I didn't feel that I deserved this hostility, and I was quite confused. It was only after I read the feedback that I realized I had been inadvertently displaying hostility towards them by giving harsh criticism. I guess it was just the way I was used to giving criticism. I didn't mean to hurt anyone's feelings, but it was just kind of the way I came across. So, I quickly had to learn how to deliver criticism in a more diplomatic way.

In doing some thinking, I came up with some of my own suggestions. Firstly, just simply being aware of my weakness gives me the opportunity to control myself when giving criticism. Secondly, I plan to request more feedback from my peers, so I can see if I'm on track. Also, I'm thinking about doing a learning contract with my facilitator, so this way I can hold myself accountable to my improvements or failures.

So far things are coming along, but sometimes, when I look back, I can't help but feel a little resentful. I often wonder if I had not identified my communication problem through peer feedback, whether I would have been able to identify the problem at all. I don't know the answer to that question, but I do know that my facilitator should have had a bigger role in helping me identify that problem. I see the facilitators as people who should be constantly observing my learning and my progress, and sometimes I feel that they're not doing a good job of it. In my opinion, my problem should have been identified by my facilitator even before receiving the peer feedback; after all, facilitators are trained to observe students, and to notice their weaknesses.

With that aside, I'm becoming more comfortable with Inquiry and my own development. From this experience, I learned something very important, even more important than communication skills actually. I learned that if I want to improve myself, I have to be conscious of it. This has become a central part of my life now. I try to do things consciously so that I can change and better myself. So I like to think that I'm constantly on the verge of a worldview shift. My worldview is constantly shifting, little bit by little bit. Where Inquiry plays into this is that perhaps it has made me more ready or more conscious of my shifting perspectives. Now, I am more eager and willing to shift my perspective when the time comes. At the end of the day, Inquiry has encouraged me to look at things from alternative perspectives and completely different paradigms.

Personally, I already feel like I'm operating from a different paradigm than I was before. And I'm going to be in a different paradigm tomorrow, because I am constantly looking at things differently. And the nice thing about Inquiry is that it supports this kind of thinking. It perhaps even encourages it.

Albert: First year, male student

Sometimes I reflect on my Inquiry experience, and I get lots of mixed feelings. For example, we have these group projects in first year, and in the first term, we thought it was a silly project. This term, we know more about what to do, and we're treating it a lot more seriously. Now, I spend a lot of time with my group. I spend a lot of time online with my group. Even during Reading Week. I'm spending a lot more time than before. I understand that everything is about process, but there's not much to show for it. Inquiry is a course where I go and do stuff, but I'm not really taking anything out of it.

I just find it frustrating not knowing where I'm going, and not sure if I'm heading in the right direction. Back in September this was one of my concerns, I didn't know what I was doing and what things were about. And even now, I'm still not too sure. I sometimes wonder if my frustrations have eased over time, but no, they're still there. But it's not that big of a concern. Now, it's about going with the flow and not worrying too much.

Was Inquiry the type of course I expected when I came into the program? Maybe something like this, but not quite. I expected a bit more structure. Not like "You can do anything you like." I didn't expect that part.

I'm not too sure if my peers have similar feelings, but I know this much. People don't take Inquiry as seriously as other courses. It's like, okay, we have a group project, I'll show up, but I don't think people are learning the same things from it. It's still mysterious. I'm not sure what we're supposed to learn about it. We gossip about it a lot. About what the facilitators want. What kind of people they are... just trying to find out what everyone else thinks about the course.

I guess we're all developing our ideas of where we're supposed to be. In my group, we all have different ideas. And convincing is needed to get people to know that process is this, and product is that, and this is what the facilitators want. Some people have the wrong idea abut Inquiry, and some just don't care enough about it. They just come in every morning, and they sit there, they listen, and then they go home.

Other people are really passionate about it. They get it. And they know that process is important. And they're there for the Inquiry idea.

Inquiry is such a big difference from high school. In grade twelve everything was about marks, marks, marks. Who cares about what you learn. So as long as I can regurgitate, it's okay, like getting a 99% was easy. Now, in Inquiry, marks don't matter. I get to set my own course load, how I wish to study... and that's really the main frustration... just getting used to the fact that it's internal learning, that we're learning for ourselves. In high school we kind of knew that, but not really. There were always the teachers, saying you must complete this or I'll do this. Now it's not like that.

I guess this change in perspective is a good thing. But I wish it could have happened gradually, maybe starting in high school, instead of having it happen all of sudden at university. I think it's a great thing, less focus on marks and more on learning. I talked to other people, for them it's about reading the textbook, memorization and multiple choice tests... and they come out of it forgetting everything. For Inquiry, you actually learn things for yourself... there are no tests... it's an awesome thing. I really enjoy Inquiry now and I like to hear what people have to say. I think others are missing out on the experience because they don't have Inquiry. It's an eye-opener for a lot of people.

Robert: 4ᵗʰ year, male student

I'm in fourth year now, and I've had some time to look back at my four years of university. Reflecting on some of my experiences, I can honestly say that my Inquiry experience definitely changed my concept of learning. In high school and even in first year it was all about lecturing. I had to memorize a bunch of facts and then I had to regurgitate it on a test. I became accustomed to that style of learning, but Inquiry changed all of that. It's funny, but once I became accustomed to Inquiry, things became easier. I remember so much more now from my Inquiry classes than I do from my lecture-based classes. For an Inquiry class, I do my own research, I search for my own answers, and I teach myself everything along the way, all of this really helps me remember the material.

It wasn't always that easy however. I was a second year transfer, so I took both first year Inquiry and second year Inquiry in my second year of university. I was simply thrown right into it, and I didn't really know what to expect. At first I was confused because the instructions were not clear, but things turned out really well at the end. When I did second year Inquiry in second semester, things really began to click for me. I remember in second year Inquiry, I did a research project on an infectious disease. If anyone were to ask me about that project, I could tell that person everything I learned verbatim. On the other hand, if that same person were to ask me questions from a lecture-based course I did in the same semester, I would not be able to recall anything.

For second year Inquiry, I had to do a presentation. The presentation was prepared by nine other students and I, and only one of us would be chosen at random to present. We were all so nervous and so scared. We were also really tired, but it all came together wonderfully. The neat thing was that we had all done our research, so even though we were nervous, we were still very prepared.

Fate would have it that I was chosen to present. And when I was presenting, I was actually presenting! I was just talking, I wasn't even reading off my notes. It was just me teaching the class what I had researched, and I felt very much like a professional lecturer. It was such a great experience.

One of my third year Inquiry classes was an amazing experience, and at first I didn't know what I was getting myself into. I ended up researching the topic of vaccines. I didn't really have a passion for vaccines before going into the course, but my facilitator was really great. We chose to look at South Africa and one sexually transmitted infection, and how if a hypothetical vaccine were to exist, how would we implement the vaccine and what kind of socio-cultural barriers we would face. In doing my research, I came across so many unexpected pieces of knowledge, and I totally wasn't expecting it. Actually, I loved it!

It was through this class that I first became interested in the sexually transmitted infection epidemic in Africa. As a result of this, I used my 3H03 thesis project to pursue my interest. I actually went to Africa last summer to study the socio-cultural aspects. I worked in a hospital. I learned a lot and I got to see everything first hand. It was incredible, the most incredible experience of my life, and it all started in Inquiry.

Because of my experience in Africa last year, I'm writing my formal thesis in that area. For my thesis, I'm researching different preventative methods and analyzing the major socio-cultural barriers to the implementation of these methods. I'm also focusing on health attitudes and behaviours, and considering that there is no cure at the moment, changing health attitudes and behaviours is really important. So it's strange, in retrospect, that it was that one class that got me thinking in a whole new way. And what's really neat about the whole thing is that it was totally unexpected.

So my advice for students is that anything is possible. All one needs is effort and passion, because opportunity is there for anyone who wants it. You just have to get out there and find something that you're passionate about, and you can make it into a project. Inquiry has definitely given me the opportunity to do that, and I would be quite a different person without my Inquiry experience.

3.5 Inquiry: Creating a Culture

[52,91,105,107] Tick-tock. With sweaty palms, your eyes dart towards one of your group members.

Tick-tock. As if on cue, the baton is passed on, and the thread of discussion continues in the final Inquiry interview evaluation.

[52,91,105,107] A culture develops whenever groups of people interact for a prolonged amount of time. Surely, a culture has emerged in the BHSc. Program. Do students embrace it? How do they feel about it? Read on to find out!

Tick-tock. Your face flushed and your mind saturated with thoughts, you contemplate the questions posed by your facilitator and search for possible responses to assist your group at any unexpected moment.

As the hands of the clock leap forward, so does your mind race to draw connections with acquired knowledge and experiences, in response to the questions spontaneously posed to your group. In what seems like hours, a typical thirty-minute assessment interview is an opportunity to share and discuss what you have learned and to evaluate your progress. In many ways, it is a moment of bonding for students. Like your fellow peers, you live and strive from challenge to challenge, driven by a shared passion for learning. As the interview draws near, you realize how far you have traveled and how much you have grown as a team, as one. You are bound by a culture of Inquiry.

The culture of Inquiry is defined and redefined in an incessant cycle by the enthusiasm of each individual student, facilitator, and administrator. Culture, from a broad perspective, encompasses the shared values and knowledge of a social group, as well as the attitudes and behavior that are characteristic of a social body or organization. In a recent paper from the United Nations Educational, Scientific, and Cultural Organization (UNESCO), an educational culture is defined as a "part and parcel of citizenship" (Candy, 2000). By establishing a culture of learning, universities play the important role of serving as a social institution for the democratization of knowledge.

All for One, and One for All

Indeed, collaboration is a core, recurring component that is key to the identification and development of the Bachelor of Health Sciences (BHSc) culture. This is reflected not only in academic activities but also in spirit-building events where students can interact on a personal level. When inquired about which elements comprise the BHSc culture, one study participant described:

> Collaborative learning. That's like the first thing that comes to mind (...). [Collaboration was formally discussed] in first year, [when] we all came together and [the assistant dean] talked to us, [and also] in second year [when we] talked about the 4X03 stuff. We have [LearnLink] as a huge tool to talk to people, talk to our whole class really, and post questions. And you know, get answers and get points of view. And I think it's a major part of our culture that we have that (...). We don't [initially] have that collaborative mind set, but it's kind of slowly being incorporated into our learning and even just our learning outside our classes and stuff, like meeting up in the lounge and discussing stuff. I think it's great.

Certainly, the program promotes diverse opportunities to foster collaboration amongst peers. Asking questions, sharing research findings, or planning future career paths, the conduit to do so is very tangible and encompassing. Although the constructs of the BHSc Program are theoretical, the concept of a close small-knit conglomeration of different individuals is very real. Despite a mosaic in culture upbringing, BHSc students were able to not only accommodate the diversity, but also maximize its potential. One student commented:

> I think [the BHSc culture] is very much built on getting to know your peers and being able to work together. A lot of our Inquiry classes are teamwork [based] as you know: small group learning and teaching each other. And if you don't know your peers then how can you teach them at the same level and how can you have such meaningful discussions or arguments even when they are good? [You cannot] learn something if you don't debate it [or] if you don't talk about it, if you don't have that interaction with others.

Learning Within and Beyond Ourselves

Whether it is through the virtual or physical community, BHSc students extend great efforts to seek possible answers for questions from a wide spectrum. It is through this collective search, and the mentality behind unraveling innovative methods and ideas, that a relatively non-competitive, intimate community setting is further strengthened.

With such typical enormous class sizes in university settings, it seems rather unlikely that competition would not be a subtle force. Yet, the small-group approach, a core element in all Inquiry classes of all years, enables students to collaborate for outcomes that are more effective. A program that emphasizes competition leads to surface learning, where knowledge is didactically imparted and students then temporarily process and regurgitate it, despite intentions to do otherwise (McAlpine, 2004); in an Inquiry classroom, the urgency and need to compete is minimized, enabling the establishment of greater trust in sharing ideas and work.

Be it the means or the end, the BHSc culture, with Inquiry as hallmark, permeates the decisions, actions, and outcomes made by its participants. Otherwise defined by experiential learning, this incessant cycle of knowledge uptake and transfer facilitates the application and expansion of Inquiry skills to realms beyond the classroom:

> Right now [I'm a fourth year peer tutor], and what we've done is we try to get ourselves exposed to more of the community. We've done stuff within our faculty, within the McMaster community, but we want to expose ourselves to the Hamilton community [as well]. We do things that are, you know, outside of the realm of science (...) that you normally wouldn't do inside the class, right? Other groups do things like, I think other groups [are] sponsoring a child; I think the class is actually trying to do that for a year. Other groups are doing things like fitness or healthy eating. The transfers are building a support group for other transfers. Basically, it [is] just time [for] getting to do what you've wanted to do but didn't have time to do throughout the other years. Basically, our class is having a chance to get us to help others in the program or at school.

Top Down, Bottom Up

[52] In creating the Inquiry culture, the support of program administration is critical. Student learning depends greatly on a program's curriculum design, values, and teaching methods, elements that should be open to evaluation and change if students are to be truly empowered. In the BHSc Program, it is not uncommon for students affect course design changes. However, this would not be possible without the support of administration, working behind the scenes to promote the flexible and creative system that is Inquiry. One participant in our ethnographic interviews captured the effect of this resource very clearly (for more on resources, turn to page 123):

> I guess the staff is there for you and that's something that [is] defining about this. And I was just amazed by the sense of community and that everyone's there for each other. That's the one thing that stands out in my mind.

Part of the structural support that is reflected in the Inquiry culture is the compassion of its instructors, facilitators, and staff. As captured in one response, in discussion about the hierarchy between students and staff:

> Yes, in particular when we're with the facilitator, it seems like we're working with the person, and not just [him or her] talking to us in a downward manner. It's almost as if they're working alongside with us, and they're helping us achieve our goals. They're not [available the entire] time, they're not always with you when you're doing your work; but whenever you have something pop up, or [if] you have a problem, you can always contact them.

Although student experiences remain unique, the underlying interactions with the individuals who constitute the academic community are shared. Inevitably, the educational philosophy found in the BHSc Program is not sustained by specific people but by the mix of personalities that work towards creating a learning community. When asked how the BHSc Program would be without Inquiry, one participant voiced, "I will never cease to [be] amazed at the number of people that are willing to help [me]." By drawing the curriculum and course purpose closer to the heart and mind, not only is there greater reflection of learning process, but also there is a strengthening of intrinsic factors that foster knowledge acquisition and curiosity. Without administrative support and facilitators preserving the ideals of Inquiry in graduating class after graduating class, students cannot establish a sustaining interest or a sense of ownership with their learning progress and product (McAlpine, 2004).

---

[52] You have just learned about how facilitators help instill values of Inquiry. This section explores how facilitators and other BHSc staff also help promote a culture of Inquiry. If you are an educator, examine how your actions shape the culture of your classroom and students. What changes would you make in your own behaviour to improve student experiences?

Is Homogeneity Definitive?

Amongst BHSc students, differing views towards the Inquiry culture do exist. While collaboration is almost an inevitable part of the program, a minority of individuals does not feel that the BHSc culture is entirely unique:

> Is there a distinct culture? I don't know. I think as a group of people, we definitely stand out. I think that over time, we start to think differently, a little bit differently as other people. [But compared to students from other programs], I think that we definitely share a lot of the same frustrations, and the same motivations, and the same sort of things that we'll get excited over, and things that we get upset over. But I think that definitely we as a group might have more tools to go through and figure things out.

Certainly, the program guides student development towards critical thinking and creativity in all their activities. Through extensive group work and alternative evaluation tools, students have a chance to explore their individuality. Students in the BHSc Program may share many common traits and academic endeavours, but to mechanically categorize them as one, and only one, group of individuals would elicit many differing opinions.

Additionally, not all students embrace the idea of self-directed learning. Although these qualities are hallmarks of Inquiry and the BHSc culture at large, it does leave some bitter taste for a minority population. When asked to describe his experience in one Inquiry course, a student responded:

> The fact that there [are] two groups [that you have to participate in] makes it a lot more work. I realize through last year and this year that, most of the time, [doing group work is] spent idly and there's really low productivity. There's one person typing, and another typing, and they read it out, and type, and then read it out again. You go through half an hour to progress through one or two sentences in a paragraph. Well, I'm exaggerating a little bit, but it's not as productive as something (...) would be [if worked on individually]. So the group thing, sure it's necessary, but at the same time, it's on the borderline of being too much.

Whether negative experiences from group work hinder progress is debatable. Given that learning for a small body of students was affected by poor group experiences, it would be beneficial to explore this issue further.

As the Seasons Change...

In transitioning between the undergraduate years, the BHSc culture has impacted the personal growth and self-understanding of many. Especially with the opportunity to pursue personal interests and projects in the senior years, students report a sense of bittersweet disengagement to it all. However, even as students branch out in later years, the program continues to provide ways of bringing them back together.

I've just... you do get a little bit removed from that BHSc culture [because there are only two required courses in fourth year]. I do not really experience the culture except [in my] 4X03 [class], and maybe some of the other courses I'm taking where I [still] see a [small] number of people [from the BHSc]. And that's [because] people are now discovering their own [paths based on] what their interests are. And it's good to still know that there are events [and opportunities which bring you back] to the BHSc culture. That's one of the big things about BHSc... the Christmas parties, the formals, those kinds of things, those are honestly what you'll remember and those are what I remember... the friends that I made and how it changes a person. (...) So as I've gone through [the years], yes I've been a little bit removed from BHSc, but still [the culture] impacts [me in some] way.

Undoubtedly, from beginning to end, BHSc students hold dear to their hearts and minds the concept of continuity, that they are not fragmented, but rather intricately connected members of a community. In this community, individuals combine their efforts, knowledge, and ideas to strive towards a vision of mutual benefit. In Inquiry, students develop an innate sense and trust in group learning, and in each other; this constitutes the very essence of the BHSc culture.

Experiences in Inquiry, with its facilitators and small classroom learning, are powerful as they can transform the linear working mind into an interactive and networking one. By amalgamating like-minded agents to form an academic community, and in doing so, sustaining the Inquiry culture, opportunities for greater communication and rapport-building are consistently facilitated.

Unconventional Approaches

An important element of the Inquiry culture is its flexible framework for students to explore multiple venues and resources in seeking answers. When asked about the process for an Inquiry final project, one participant provided a particularly intriguing description:

I would use the *Meducator* as an example, that is a publication that is produced by McMaster students, [through which] undergrad[ate] students had the opportunity to research things and present it for publication. That particular project is very product-oriented, you're essentially writing and presenting to other people. But the process itself takes a lot of the things that we learned in Inquiry, like formulating a question and going about answering it, with little to no help from other people. That's like what we were taught in Inquiry. (...) So it really depends on how far the student wishes to run with the tools that he's been given.

Box 3.2
BHSc Learning Opportunities: The Meducator

The Meducator is a seasonal health sciences student-run journal providing opportunities for article publication for students of all years. It is a Health Sciences initiative and combines the efforts of BHSc students, supervisors of students' research, and numerous Faculty of Health Sciences staff for consultations.

By applying the skill set of Inquiry[26] with the forum to realize creative ideas, students not only master the process of problem-solving but also the skills to integrate knowledge to its real-life context. Whether it is seeking the advice of an expert in the field, participating in a lecture series, or transferring summer work experiences into an Inquiry initiative, the options are diverse and intriguing. In creating the Inquiry culture, the environment for lifelong learning is fostered. Besides students being regarded as autonomous agents of learning, there is also the recognition that knowledge acquisition can occur at any age in formal, non-formal and informal settings (Candy, 2000). You have literally the world in your hands, the choice to pursue answers in the format of a textbook, a specialist, a patient, or your parents. Why not challenge yourself and take your questions a step farther, beyond the classroom and beyond the parameters of comfort?

According to UNESCO, education should promote the intrinsically motivated and satisfied individual to systematically acquire, renew, and evaluate knowledge, skills, and attitudes as they modify with changes in the surrounding social environment (Candy, 2000). Inquiry, with its flexibility that encourages students to expand their learning methods and to "think outside the box," establishes the critical conduit towards lifelong learning. The feeling that, as students, they are able to decide their own learning path has helped form the overarching culture of Inquiry. This feeling of empowerment is imprinted on many of the students, and facilitates the feeling that they will be able to affect the world, in small and large ways.

---

[26] Curious to learn more about this skill set? Turn to page 26!

3.6 Group Work and Collaboration

[100,118][107] Two heads are better than one. We've understood the truth behind this phrase for a while, but another phrase, easier said than done, often comes to our defense.

Group work is not easy.[38, 88] What makes it even more challenging is that there is no magical formula to create a dynamic and effective group. Each group has its own strengths, weaknesses, and personalities that make up the group. Even the simplest decisions can sometimes take hours to agree on. You have to put in the time, have patience, and be open-minded in order to reap the benefits. Take a moment to jot down what group work means to you:

When we think of group work, we often think of business professionals in their luxurious and well-appointed boardrooms. In reality though, we are surrounded by group work and opportunities for collaboration and discussion. Take your family, for instance, or even a close group of friends. Although we may not realize it, both of these are avenues in which we use many of the essential skills needed for group work and collaboration. Whether it is arriving at a decision about what to order for dinner, which movie to watch, or how to put together a bed from *Ikea*, we collaborate with the people around us.

Though the skills needed for group work and collaboration are similar, a difference exists between the definitions of these two processes. Group work and collaboration both imply working with others; however, group work does not necessarily mean that individuals are working cooperatively or towards the

---

[100,118] How do students feel about working in a group? What conflicts arise and how do they deal with them? Read on to find out!

[107] You just learned the ways in which students use Learnlink to communicate and collaborate. This section will reveal the dynamics of group work and other modes of communication.

[38, 88] I hate my group and never want to see their ugly faces again, or hear their annoying incessant complaining and negative thinking. I would rather pull my hair out than work with them! FRUSTRATION: it is a key element to all group processes. Sometimes it can be overcome. Sometimes it just has to be endured. Turn to page 38 to read about other students' experiences with the dragon of frustration in group work and learn some tips to deal with it. Or, if you are looking to explore the other side of the spectrum, group success, turn to page 88.

same goal. Collaboration on the other hand, occurs when members of the group cooperate and work towards a shared goal or outcome (Johnson & Johnson, 1999).

Starting in first year, BHSc students experience an abundance of collaborative projects. Many of these students come with the belief that independent work is far more effective than being in a group. The reasons why students may feel this way are quite diverse. They may have had negative experiences working with others, they may not have the communication skills or confidence needed to work in a group, or they may perceive group work as tedious and a waste of time. It should also be noted that most students have come from a curriculum that promotes individual work and rewards students for right answers. Over time though, they appreciate the importance of working with others. The ability to plan, discuss, teach one another, rework, and reorganize becomes an essential survival skill. One student describes the effect group work has had on them:

> I think it's just made me see that there is no one point of view; that on any topic, you're always going to have people that disagree for (...) very valid reasons. (...) I think it's about working with those people and accepting that you're not always going to be on the same page as those people, but that (...) doesn't necessarily mean that you can't work together, that you can't learn from each other, and you can't still hold your beliefs. As long as you just accept that there are differences out there and differences of opinion.

Working in a group is effective not only for the range of ideas and perceptions that can be heard, but also for the development of skills that can be applied to other contexts. These include communication skills, leadership skills, presentation skills, and being able to reflect upon and evaluate strengths and weaknesses. Many students explained that group work is an essential life skill:

> Group work is amazing and very important for all students because (...) when you go out into the work field, you will be working with other people. You have to know how to properly interact, consider other people's opinions, and be very mindful of all those things. I felt that (...) the group work [in Inquiry] is a great thing. (...) I love interacting with other people to work on the same sort of topic.

In the BHSc Program, students use each other as a main resource by which they construct and integrate knowledge. One student describes the struggle they experienced and the satisfaction that followed when the group was able to integrate all the concepts on a particular topic:

> There was a group of 10 of us in second term of last year doing (...) research and we had tons of information, like hours and hours of information. It was about five or six days until we had to present, and it was the 30-minute presentation where one student's name is picked out of a hat and they have to present. (...) So we had tons of information, but for some reason, we could not put our fingers on why none of it was fitting together. Nothing was coming together,

and it was just [that] we worked all term, we found out all this information, we found all these pieces... but for some reason, it's just not coming together (...). There [were] about seven or eight laptops in the room, [and we were] researching this and researching that (...). Everyone was just running around like chickens with their heads cut off (...). So we stopped. (...) We just said, okay, put everything down and let's just get together (...) and we're going to look at the pieces we have and try to fit it together and see what's missing. We went and got a sheet of paper and a pencil, and we just started making a diagram of what's going on (...). And we realized that there was one piece missing. And we're like, why is this happening? (...) What's the connection? So because of that, because of just getting everyone together and reflect[ing], (...) we were actually able to go on, research, and find what was missing. And everything was just clear at that point and we made this awesome diagram for the presentation. (...) That was probably (...) one of the best moments because we had been together at that point for maybe 9 or 10 hours working on this presentation, and to have that moment (...) of clarity where everything made sense. So it was perfect.

Despite its importance in the BHSc Program, there are a few students who do not develop the drive or passion for group work. One student described his experiences:

I often worked with people whom I would normally not interact with. I was forced to not only interact, but also work towards a common goal [with] people with very different ideologies from mine, and with very different social, cultural, and ethnic backgrounds. Indeed, my previous experience caused me to often disagree with the direction in which other group members wanted to go and, often, despite voicing my opinion, I would go along with other's ideas for the sake of peace within the group. This, in and of itself, is not necessarily conducive to good learning.

One of the main reasons that group work and collaboration is embraced in the BHSc Program is that it has synergistic results. Although each team you are a part of may have different dynamics, there are a few fundamentals which help to foster group work and collaboration. First and foremost, a comfortable and safe environment must be created whereby members of the group feel that they are able to freely express their thoughts and ideas. Essentially, the element of trust must be established and given priority. Everyone's ideas must be treated equally and members of the group should be responsive and supportive of others' contributions. The notion of positive interdependence must also be woven into a group. This means that members of the group should feel that they are responsible for and dependent on the rest of the group's performance. In a true collaborative environment, the group should be working together to achieve a common goal. This type of atmosphere promotes group learning and provides a "safe playground" where team members can build off each other's ideas, brainstorm and drive creativity, while at the same time developing skills of cooperation, decision-making, organization and communication. Effective groups promote reasoning, critical thinking, and organization and integration of information; additionally, groups members should accommodate, accept, and encourage each other's ideas. The BHSc Program also provides its students with a number of resources that aid in group learning. One of these resources is LearnLink. This electronic resource serves as an online forum where students can share knowledge and ideas with their team members

We've provided you with the fundamentals of working in groups, but knowing how to manage conflicts is just as important. With so many different people working together and so many ideas on the table, it is sometimes natural to push your idea ahead of others. This creates unnecessary tensions and often hostility within the group. Other times, some group members may not be producing as much work as the rest of their team. Personal accountability, where each person is responsible for completing a set number of tasks and working towards achieving group goals, is essential. How do you tell a group member they are not contributing as much as other members of the team? How do you tell a group member that they are leading the discussion and not letting other opinions surface? There are no concrete answers to these questions or a "how to" guide that will tell you how to handle the sensitive issues that arise when working with others. Providing constructive criticism is often one of the most difficult skills to develop when working in groups. This skill is developed over time and through practice. Often, the ability to work effectively in a group comes from being open-minded and understanding:

> Everyone has something they can put on the table, but it's about telling them what your opinions are, and what you expect from everyone, and what they should be expecting from you. By getting that on the table, you're more likely to live up to the expectations that others have of you and you become more understanding of the limitations of your group, like people not being able to make it to meetings. You are able to co-exist and work together more efficiently (...) because everyone in your group is here for a reason, and you have to find what it is that they can contribute to the group. If there's an area they are not strong in, it should be expected that other individuals will come in and pick up that slack. If someone is not that great at writing, that person could be the overseer of that writing process. You want to expose people who are not good at writing to the process so that they can improve. Also, you want to ensure that the final product is of as high quality as possible. That was my new perspective of group work after walking into [Inquiry], being able to adapt to new group situations.

There is no doubt that there are emotional processes that groups go through when working together. On top of that, skills such as communication and organizing and integrating information are vital. Very often, students feel that the most important skills they have developed over the years are communication skills, learning how to handle yourself in groups, and how to use group work to advance your learning:

I would say that my greatest Inquiry achievement would be the fact that being put into a group, I've been able to improve my communication among the group by being able to speak up in situations where I normally wouldn't, being able to express my views, (...) opinions, and thoughts. (...) In BHSc, because everything is group-based, and you are put into all these different groups, there comes a point where you get so comfortable with the group and with the group setting (...). As that happens, you feel more and more comfortable expressing your thoughts. And as the same time, you can keep it professional. (...) We all have a goal to get towards; it's not like we're meeting just to have fun or anything like that. We all have a project; we all have some sort of research that we have to do. That is (...) our group goal. (...) Everybody who has thoughts or opinions that they want to express can [contribute to the group goal]. And I view that by being able to [contribute] in a group setting has helped me a lot because this was something that I wasn't used to. I think that's a very big achievement for myself, to be able to voice my opinions in a group setting, to be able to lead a group discussion, to be able to direct a group (...) [towards] a direction that I want to go into, and at the same time, get other people's opinions. And when I get other people's opinions, I can refine my opinions. Maybe I didn't think about that. Maybe I like their opinions better. I feel that's been my greatest achievement.

The above quotation shows that group work is a process. [85]⅃Students' comfort and ability to approach group learning improves over time and with practice. Students realize that group learning can be a source for personal growth, academic development, and formation of friendships. Students also expressed that working in groups provided them with motivation and inspiration:

I volunteered (...) [at an organization designed to help individuals who are homeless] with another student in my small group, an individual whom I have, since then, considered to be one of my best friends. I had (...) very narrow-minded views about homelessness, but my opinions were drastically altered (...) following my real-life experience [with the homeless]. Witnessing the compassion of one of my peers caused me to take time to consider how ignorant my own views had been, and to open my mind up to new possibilities. It was an amazing learning experience which I'll never forget.

Many students have taken group work and collaboration outside the classroom and have experienced personal growth and a sense of accomplishment as a result. Since conflict of ideas and personalities is sometimes an inevitable feature of working in groups, it is important to be able to recognize and evaluate problems that surface and use open discussion to solve them. Without open dis-

---

[85]⅃ Group work doesn't have to be half-bad! In fact, the Inquiry Book Team worked pretty well together! Actually, somebody get out some Queen because I'm pretty sure we need to sing We Are The Champions on top of tables after that last Inquiry presentation. TRIUMPHS. They happen sometimes, when you least expect it. After the frustration and the struggle, sometimes, things just click. Here are some stories of other students' great success stories that might just inspire you.

cussion, conflicts can easily intensify and negatively affect the performance of the group. Problems are often spotted when reflecting on process and performing self and peer assessments. One student reflects:

> [My experience in Inquiry] has also taught me the value of group work, and given me the experience of dealing with group conflict. (...) I have had a forum to develop and improve both intrapersonal and interpersonal skills that will be especially essential in the years to follow. Within the group, conflicts arose quite often as people had different perspectives on the topic and saw the project going in different directions. Yet, bit by bit, each of us learned to compromise, to pull his or her weight, and to define a common group goal. And in the end, it all worked out. Disagreements were for the most part settled. We actually started to enjoy the group meetings, which were long and usually quite difficult to schedule, and all the semester's hard work had paid off.

Just as conflicts should be recognized and discussed, successes and achievements of the group should be celebrated. After all, groups should be proud of their accomplishments. In building an open line of communication and a level of comfort with each other, many students perceive each other as their most valued resource:

> [Inquiry] fosters an appreciation for how valuable your peers can be in the learning process. (...) Inquiry experiences have taught me the true value of group work, and just how much others can contribute to my personal learning experience. Inquiry has reinforced the merits of using peers as a resource in the learning process.

Apart from the academic development that occurs in groups, students also find that group work allows them to learn more about people and form friendships:

> In every group, you end up learning about the people, not just the topic, but learning about each individual in your group, and become closer friends. After that group, you may or may not ever talk to them again, depending on your interests or whatever, but during that time you get to learn something about the people in the [program]. I think that's nice.

The above quotation shows that students are responsible for each other's learning, growth and experience. Although facilitators help students through the experience, they take the back seat and allow students to work through the process themselves, allowing them to sink and swim together.[46, 51]

[46, 51] As you can see, facilitation is really important in terms of student development. To learn more about the role of a facilitator, turn to page 46. But if you want to see some examples of how facilitators interact with and help students learn, turn to page 51.

Group work and collaboration has undoubtedly become a pivotal part of the BHSc culture. The small class sizes help foster the intimacy needed for students to engage in active group work and experience the frustrations and triumphs associated with it.[79, 37, 71]

[79, 37, 71] The emotions and close ties that are associated with small group learning often go along with an entire learning "culture" associated with that environment. To consider the culture that exists in the BHSc Program, turn to page 79. As well, the existence of a learning culture brings with it strong emotional bonds to all those who are involved in the culture. To see reflections on the emotions that are common to Inquiry learning, turn to page 37. Or you can also turn to page 71 and read some personal stories of students' experiences in the BHSc Program.

Topic 4: The Tool Box

4.1 Resources of Inquiry

[28] How do educational resources contribute to a positive learning experience? What are some resources that help you learn in your own life?

Growth is inherent in the life cycle of living things. However, some environments foster enhanced development. A plant with the right amount of sunshine and care, tailored to its individual needs, will grow to its full potential. Students, much like plants, will grow into life-long learners in environments that provide the appropriate tools to foster development. The BHSc Program provides several of such tools to its undergraduates. How do these resources serve students? The following quotation introduces what we found:

> The resources made available to me by BHSc have positively affected my experiences at McMaster. For example, anatomy lab specimens [and] simulated

---

[28] You are here because of your curiosity to learn about resources as a whole in the BHSc Program. Enjoy!

patient interviews have allowed (...) hands-on practice and application of knowledge, aid[ing] in the development of practical skills (e.g. communication) and the long-term retention of the material. The BHSc staff has also been most helpful and supportive, which goes a long way when you get stuck on an academic problem, when you need help pulling off an event, when you have a personal problem, or when you just want to share your progress and successes. I am also grateful for the BHSc lounge, with all of its technology and recreational equipment, which provide a comfortable atmosphere conducive to socializing, group work, and individual research.

Facilitators

For many students, facilitators act as an important learning resource:

I think the facilitators are a wonderful resource. They know a lot more than we do, and they do help us out (...). They know their material for sure. (...) When we have a meeting, they obviously try to help you out. When we have questions, I'm never hesitant to ask them. [They may know the answer themselves but] if they want you to figure [it] out for yourself, (...) [they ask] another question that will help [you] answer the original question.

Resources like facilitators and professors (...) have affected my experiences at McMaster. Not only because there are a lot of engaging and enthusiastic teachers among them, but because it's built into our curriculum. (...) We get to sit down with some of them to talk and get honest, constructive feedback. They provide a bit of direction to one's learning, and the sense of security that comes with that is much appreciated.

The facilitators [are] a resource to get more resources.

There is no doubt that facilitators are the backbone of first year Inquiry. They are a critical resource to students experiencing the ups and downs of Inquiry. Facilitators help students overcome barriers to growth and celebrate epiphanies with one another. They also offer their expertise, guidance, and feedback to students, not just on academic issues, but on anything meaningful, like their futures. As one student demonstrates:

I have just recently begun talking about my future options with some of the members of the Health Science Faculty and I wish I [had] used their knowledge in the past. The members have helped me plan and discuss my future and interests and have helped guide me.

Students also expressed that facilitators provide feedback, and that they cater to the learning needs of individuals.

What I also like about BHSc is how we can approach our faculty. (...) We can ask any questions at almost any time. If we have issues, we can always go and talk to them and they will try to solve the issues. Also, [I] like how they have the ability to provide feedback. They can change the course, in the middle of the course, in the middle of the situation. It is excellent. In my human movement [class], some of us were giving [our facilitator] feedback and she was immediately [responded], "This is what you guys are saying, this is what I have to say... lets try to do *this* now." It's awesome for a [professor] to hear what you have to say.

And that's another thing, the facilitators (...) are much more accepting of new ideas. [It is an attitude of], "Well, I don't have [your] answer down, but now that I think about it, you have a point." (...) So that sort of atmosphere (...) is more friendly and inviting in that way.

Heck, they'll take you out for a beer if that's what you need to learn!"

The resourcefulness and availability of facilitators can be accredited in some part to the small class size. Some students feel that this proximity helps their interaction with the facilitators and is cause for comfort.

[I] think [class size] makes a huge difference [in determining facilitator availability]. In all my [non-Inquiry] classes, you don't see the professor up close. If [I] have a question, I am really hesitant to ask it. They haven't seen my face and they don't know who I am. But in [my Inquiry] classes, it's small [and my facilitators] probably know who [I am] and [so there is] a lot more interaction. I feel a lot more comfortable asking questions.

I can't put into words how much I appreciate the personal aspect of the program. The small classes are definitely a great opportunity to get to know your peers and facilitators; you know each one on a first name basis. It's not like it's a [class of 600] and you never speak to your professor the whole time you're there, and you know who he is but he has no clue who you are. I've definitely taken advantage of the (...) personal aspect of it.

The fact that we have such a small number of students, we're able to potentially build a relationship with [our] professors, if necessary. Some students will, some students don't, but more importantly, since there is such a small number, professors are welcoming in meeting with students and helping students one-on-one if possible. [In contrast], I'm taking a (...) course right now, where there's (...) over 500 students in the class and it's impossible for the professor to take emails. So the professor (...) said on the first day of class, "Don't send me emails, I won't respond to them." I think that (...) the ability to interact with our teachers (...) is a huge benefit to our learning. [46]

Peer tutors
[30] A new university, new home, new friends, and a new program, it seems

---

[46] To learn more about the role of a facilitator in student learning turn to page 46.
[30] First-year students often have many unanswered questions about peer tutors: Are they friends or teachers? Can I tell them things? Why do they keep asking me what I think? Consider this crazy conundrum while reading more about peer tutors.

that nothing is the same. On top of that, you step into a twilight zone where marks are non-existent, questions come by the truckloads, and answers are no-where to be found! In all the confusion and despair comes the helping hand of a peer tutor, under the guidance of whom you may find some solace of knowing that you are not alone, others have gone through the same process and have suc-ceeded. The enthusiasm, competence, and success which peer tutors model help students feel more self-confident. Students that are peer-tutored experience greater self-confidence, sense of responsibility, improvement in organizational skills, and the advancement of interpersonal skills. In clinical practice, peer teaching has been found to ease anxiety, increase confidence, and improve skills in critical thinking and management (Owens et al., 2001).

Traditionally, it was thought that tutors should be the "better students" who are mini-versions of the instructor; the hierarchy in knowledge would thus go from instructor (at the top), to peer tutor, and finally to student. However, cur-rent research suggests that a unique interaction exists between tutors and stu-dents altogether, which is not necessarily comparable to instructor-student inter-actions. According to this new view, tutors should be more realistic, proximate, and credible models to students (Topping, 2005).

In the BHSc Program, 4th year students are tutors for a group consisting of four or five first year Inquiry students. Tutoring in Inquiry is poles apart from traditional courses in terms of structure. In traditional courses, where a struc-tured curriculum must be learned, peer tutors reinforce and help students apply the material already delivered by the professor. They often have specified roles and they receive training relevant to the discipline being taught. However, In-quiry does not have a structured curriculum. There is no specific subject matter which must be learned. It is the method of learning which must be absorbed and practiced by the students; tutors help strengthen this effort. Facilitators often provide students with the freedom to determine their own learning, allowing them to wander in any direction they choose. This allows students to stray from beaten paths, think creatively, and try new things. During this process, peer tu-tors help students navigate by guiding with questions which help them under-stand what it is they are learning and why.[46,26] In doing so, not only do students have a greater appreciation for the issues currently examined, but they also be-come aware of new opportunities for growth.

> You bounce a question off of [peer tutors] and they might give you a straight-forward answer [or] they might not. But they do a good job of guiding you.

> The best kind of resource I think is the peer tutor. A good peer tutor (…) can

---

[46,26] Even though peer tutors and facilitators have similar goals, they have different roles! To explore the role of the facilitator, turn to page 46. Peer tutors are unique be-cause they have already gone through the first year Inquiry experience and have been developing their skill sets over the past four years. To learn more about the Inquiry skill set, check out page 26.

really give you a direction, and I think that's what a lot of people are kind of concerned about with Inquiry, [the importance of a direction].

Inquiry peer tutors are not responsible for providing grades or marks. Grading may create an atmosphere of discomfort for the learner (Topping 2005). Tutors assess group progress and provide feedback to students. They also receive feedback and self-evaluate their own learning. Exchanging feedback is more cognitively demanding and thus, has more learning benefits (Topping 2005). Through feedback, tutors help students identify their strengths and weaknesses and subsequently improve upon them.

> When I asked [my peer tutor] about Inquiry problems, he pretty much helped me realize, "Okay, I guess I am doing the right thing. (...) I guess I am on the right track."

> [My peer tutors have given] me (...) very good, very insightful feedback.

Peer tutors not only aid academic initiatives, but also help to create an atmosphere of respect, comfort and ingenuity. They listen actively, participate, and uphold an atmosphere of respect and openness. This environment allows students to voice their concerns and ideas.

> I went to [my peer tutor] because I had some issues with second year Inquiry and asked him a few questions. I said this is what we're doing, this is what we want to look for (...). [His guidance] was really helpful to me because it gave me some insight. [My peer tutor] also came in handy when there was a conflict, and I went to him to talk to him (...). It was really helpful for me that I was able to talk to someone.
> I felt that I had more resources in terms of not just (...) textbooks, but in terms of being able to talk to faculty and peer tutors, even. When I was a [second year] transfer, we had peer tutors we could talk to, and they're there to help us. They've done it all before (...).

Tutoring does not help only students. It also benefits the peer tutors themselves. They have their own learning goals which they work to accomplish through the facilitation of students. In BHSc, the functions of the peer tutor such as paying attention, identifying discrepancies, directing students, and correcting mistakes bring benefits for the tutor as well as the group. They also develop transferable skills such as compassion, communication, self-evaluation, and the ability to give and receive feedback. One of the most important skills that both the group and tutor develop is communication as they continuously listen, explain, question, hypothesize, appraise and evaluate: Inquiry skills which apply to any aspect of life. The fourth year students who were peer tutors provided some evidence of this:

> It's good being a student facilitator with students, and I think that's why they do have peer tutors, and it's very, very beneficial. And I know how tough

it is because I'm doing it. The students are at their own pace; they're like "we might need you in certain respects, we might not need you in other respects." You feel kind of like you're vulnerable, like "You know what? I don't know if I'm doing my job right. I don't want to set them up for some sort of failure as they move on." So it's tough and it's good. I've appreciated what everyone's done and it's good that I'm getting (...) that experiential knowledge with how facilitators interact with their students.

One of the things I'm doing right now is I'm a (...) peer tutor for a [first year] Inquiry class. So that is a different experience altogether, because they're first years. [I]'ve been [through first year Inquiry before] but I'm finding that it's still pretty tough because [I'm now interacting with] different people. They're much younger, that's one thing I'm finding, [in terms of] maturity level, and getting so much Inquiry at once. They're getting the new [Inquiry-based] biology course, they're getting Inquiry, they're getting psychobio[logy].

We've gone through all this and we know they're getting bombarded with Inquiry. (...) For me, if I look at (...) first year [Inquiry], I didn't know what it was about either, right? (...) To multiply that by three or four, that's tough in itself. It's just a shock, right? So (...) if I look at my role, I just want to be a support there for (...) [the students]. If they have any questions, I don't want to just give a blanket statement that, "Oh, it'll be alright" you know? (...) If they have any questions, I'm there to help. So taking that, I'm actually continuing on with my communication skills interest. [Additionally], I'm actually a peer tutor for [a third year] communication skills class as well, so I'm almost taking the course a second time (...). I'm finding [things] a lot different from a peer tutor's aspect on the course. And I feel like I can contribute a little bit more because it is more skills-[based] and knowledge-based.

Group Work

As humans, we are constantly interacting with those around us. In doing so, people leave imprints on our minds and we leave impressions on others. Collaboration and co-operation when working with others enhance learning. Research and information analysis can be conducted individually but group work provides the opportunity to share ideas, enhance communication skills, and receive feedback. Group work is an essential skill regardless of the context within which it is used.

Do you remember the trip which you had planned for yourself?[23] Now, imagine that you had to plan your trip to your dream destination with your family members, friends, or some colleagues. How would it be different? Would you rather plan it individually or with a group of people?

---

[23] If you have not yet completed the exercise "Plan your own trip", please turn to page 23 before proceeding further.

```
┌─────────────────────────────────────────────────────────────────┐
│                                                                   │
│                                                                   │
│                                                                   │
│                                                                   │
│                                                                   │
│                                                                   │
└─────────────────────────────────────────────────────────────────┘
```

Perhaps, this reflection has provided you with an opportunity to examine your concept of group work. The BHSc Program benefits from the luxury of having a small number of students (approximately 180 per year) and adequate resources. In BHSc classes, Inquiry, psychobiology and cell biology for example, students have many opportunities to work in groups.[30] The group sizes range from 5 to 9 people, approximately. Students work in groups to complete projects relevant to the topic of study. In first year Inquiry, for example, a group is provided with a trigger which is used to define a question or a problem. The students work together to answer their question and satisfy their personal learning objectives.[24] Group work allows interaction among students and a mix of perspectives and approaches to influence learning.

> Before taking Inquiry courses, I believed that I could function better as an individual acquiring knowledge than as a member of a group. Inquiry experiences have taught me the true value of group work, and just how much others can contribute to my personal work experience. Inquiry has reinforced the merits of using peers as a resource in the work process.

Group work aids in the development of personal skills. Students become better listeners, gain confidence to participate in discussions, and practice exchanging constructive feedback. Said one student, "My group members helped me a lot to develop skills. We worked together and that helped me a lot."

Group work may not always make everyone happy. There are some challenges accompanying group work which must be dealt with in order to reap the benefits of a collaborative approach, a valuable skill for BHSc students.[85]

Library Personnel

It is your first day at the health sciences library, where literally thousands of books and journals are arranged on hundreds of stacks that tower over you. They create a maze of twists and turns; for a traveler with no compass, all hope of reaching the destination (a book) is lost. Suddenly, a librarian comes to your rescue, helping you to not only retrieve your book but also learn how to navigate the world of library resources. Usually, there are librarians available at the front

---

[30] If you want to learn more about these classes, turn to page 30.

[24] Turn to page 24 to understand the Inquiry process.

[85] To learn more about group work, collaboration, and conflict resolution as experienced by BHSc students, turn to page 85.

desk to assist students with their questions and/or concerns. They help students navigate around the library.

> We have to do a lot of research. So in the library, there are a lot of resources you can find at the circulation desk. I find that the people sitting at the circulation desk are very helpful. If there's something you are looking for, that you can't find, either if you can't find a journal downstairs or if the e-journal portal is not working, they try their best to help you out.

So you have learned how to locate the book or journal that you wanted. There is much more to research, however, than simply being able to find a book. How do you know which book you want? What if you are doing a literature search for a project? How do you find the articles you need from those hundreds of stacks and millions of articles available online? How do you know which ones are peer reviewed? Which database is the best for which subjects? How do you use those databases the right way? How do you specify the question? Fortunately, the BHSc Program has employed a librarian for helping BHSc students.

Box 4.1

The BHSc Librarian

The librarian aids student research in various ways:
- demonstrates appropriate sources of information including books and journals relevant to the subject area
- presents in BHSc classes ranging from Inquiry to Bioethics
- illustrates the most efficient methods to retrieve relevant information from journal databases, Internet websites, or library books
- illustrates how to assess and evaluate retrieved information in order to ensure credibility.

The library personnel play an important role in enhancing the research skills of students which are key to the progression of the Inquiry process according to the IREC model.[24] Several students commented on the value of such a resource to their learning:

> It was (...) the first week [of the first semester of first year when] we had to find an article for [our] psychobio[logy] essay. And we had to use [the search databases] Ovid and Pubmed. We've been using Pubmed all term; that's part of why we don't have a bio[logy] textbook. We had a lot of research skills I think. (...) We had the librarian come and tell us about where to find things, how to use the library well. And that was really helpful, I found, because we are doing so much independent research for coursework.

---

[24] Turn to page 24 to understand the Inquiry process.

I learned to use PubMed (...) from the librarian. And she did show me how to use it, and what it was good for, and that kind of thing.

I learned the value of [...] PubMed and libraries (...). I think, I still have a lot of work to do in that area, especially working in libraries. Because [of this], I have scheduled an appointment with the library person.

Students also benefit by saving time and gaining satisfaction for the credibility of the sources. They can directly access appropriate journal databases, which provide current and relevant information. By catering to one of the core principles of Inquiry, research, the library is an asset to student learning.

The BHSc Office
When you hear the word office, what do you think of?

Perhaps, you thought of computers, chairs, tables, secretaries and busy people. The BHSc students thought this:

I went to the office the other day to meet with [one of the office staff] about academic counseling and she answered some questions I had. [She] gave me some general information which was quite helpful. [The experience] was simple [and] easy. I just sent her [a message] on LearnLink; she responded and gave me a time. [She] has, I think, (...) an open-door policy on certain days. So that's available to us. [Additionally], I have met with my Inquiry facilitators out of class [in the BHSc office].

I think that the "people resources" that BHSc offers its students have contributed to my generally positive university experience. It is wonderful to know that there are approachable individuals working for the program who can assist and support you with your concerns and choices. I doubt any other program at McMaster could match the level of support provided by the BHSc administration.

The resources made available to me through BHSc have definitely affected my experience at McMaster, mostly as a framework of support for my education. Through the BHSc, I've been able to explore and educate myself on career opportunities that I never knew existed. Just recently I attended a career counseling session with office personnel and gained some real insight on what I can do with my BHSc undergraduate degree. This certainly enables me to feel more confident about my future.

I think one of the strongest benefits is the office staff. I don't think that every student has had much interaction with the staff. But me personally, I've had a lot of interaction with the office staff, and they're extremely supportive in helping a student to learn, and not just learn in terms of education and getting good grades, but just learn in terms of life skills. And I feel (...) we can sit down with [the associate dean of our program] and have a coffee with him if we want. But it's not just the associate dean in that office; there's (...) [other staff] that are so helpful, and so supportive, and so welcoming. And I mean, I just think it's great. You know you're not in this alone, which is a huge thing in university because a lot of the time, students feel like they're out there, they're alone, and they're fighting this battle on their own. Whereas I feel [that] with that office staff, there's (...) a supportive network right behind us, always working with us and supporting us.

The BHSc office is there not only to help and to process administrative tasks, such as 3H03 proposals or scholarship applications, but they also provide answers to any questions.[30] There are many resources pertaining to future goals; they provide information about post-graduate programs and meet with students to discuss any relevant issues. Staff holds open hours so that students may approach them uninhibited. Students are welcomed in with smiling faces of staff that are willing to help. The quotations above have demonstrated the accessibility of the people in the office as well as the comfortable and approachable environment available to the students. However, like the other resources available to students, the BHSc office is only as useful as the students make it.

I think that [the BHSc office] definitely [is] a good thing to have (...) available. It's a good opportunity for people to go. I just don't think that I have made use of the BHSc office staff that much. I mean there are a couple [of staff members] that I know more on a personal level, because they directed my classes [as Inquiry facilitators]. Other than that, I don't really use them. I don't ask them about future careers. I kind of do it more on my own, rather than ask them for help.

Physical Resources
A key physical resource used by BHSc students is the BHSc lounge. Here is what one student had to say:

I think [it's] wonderful. I was in there. I'm [not] there quite often, but you know, whenever I need to use it, it's very accessible. I like how it's not just a big study room. I like [that] there's always something going on, someone watching TV, someone playing a game. I was there one night and a group came in, and I instantly just started up a conversation. It's really, really easy. And I

---

[30] To discover the nature of 3H03 and other BHSc courses, turn to page 30.

like how it's for both leisure and study purposes. I know a lot of our group meetings are in there as well. I don't think it really disrupts the people [who are] studying as well. I like how you eventually see people [and] you [start] talk[ing] to people.

The BHSc lounge is a student space with computers, Internet access, meeting rooms, couches, chairs, a television, a DVD player, and a pool table. It is available 24/7 for student use. Based on the described features, how do you think the lounge impacts student learning?

The BHSc lounge serves a variety of purposes for the students. It acts as a working space, a meeting area, and a relaxation venue. Many students like a casual working area; thus, the lounge is a perfect spot for them to work individually or as a group. There are often peers available, to ask for help, or just to chat. The students acknowledge the presence of these resources as a valuable aid in their learning:

> The lounge is a great place to study and have group meetings. I think [the lounge] brings everyone together. The lounge is good because you'll always have a good computer and stuff like that. And there [are] always people. (...) It's [a] meeting spot [and] you can't always find meeting spots on campus. (...) [Since] you have so much group stuff [available], it's like the lounge is where you spend most of your time.

> [The] availability of computers in the BHSc lounge has also affected my experience (...) at McMaster because it has assured me that resources are always available to aid me in my learning.

Many students emphasize the social advantages of having a lounge. It is one place where BHSc students from all years can mingle together, strengthening the sense of community prevalent in the BHSc Program.

> [A] lot of people go to the lounge and so you can meet [them] just [by] going [there]. (...) BHSc is a pretty small program to begin with. (...) So to have things like these, it really helps to enforce that, to help enforce the sense of community.

> Many resources are available in the lounge and [they] make it possible to form relationships with not only students in your year, but those in upper and lower years as well.

The bonding which occurs between the students helps to enhance their learning. Since students have the opportunity to meet and be familiar with many faces in the Program, when they engage in group work, they are not strangers to each other.

> I think [the BHSc lounge is] great. You talk to people in other faculties and they're like "Wow! Your lounge is so cool" or "You have such a cool program." And I think it's hugely different [compared to other programs] in that [the BHSc Program] lets the students do a lot with each other. They facilitate that group environment, that collaboration. I think that providing stuff like the lounge gives us [all] the opportunity to collect in a larger area, which is good.

The lounge is a resource that contributes to the enhancement of student learning and BHSc culture in general.[79] It provides a comfortable atmosphere for students to come together for work and play. It is also known as Home Base, a name that suits its function.

Health Science Library
What are the elements you would like to see in a library? What do you use a library for?

Books, journals, computers, meeting rooms, cubicles, group study tables, photocopy machines, printers, and library personnel: are these some of the elements you imagined in your ideal library? If so, then you've just pictured the health sciences library at McMaster University. It is a library conducive to the needs of a curious learner.

> I find that the resources at McMaster, such as the libraries' e-resources, have contributed to my learning and positive experience these past few years.

There are books, journals, and multimedia available on virtually all areas of health sciences, from psychology to human reproduction, from medical education to epidemiology. The university provides access to a range of electronic resources, including e-journal databases such as Ovid Medline, Pubmed, EM-

---

[79] To learn more about BHSc culture, turn to page 79.

BASE, CINAHL, and ERIC. These allow students to find relevant information easily.

Research skills and the ability to appraise the validity and credibility of sources of information are greatly emphasized by the Inquiry approach to learning. BHSc students engage in research projects from the beginning of their first term in university. With continuous practice, they are able to refine their research skills over the years.

> First year in psychobio[logy], we [learned to become] really good at getting the journals, and the electronic journal access. That really helped because it was absolutely essential for second year Inquiry. But a lot of people might not know how to use that kind of thing, and now we're really used to [it], so it's second nature now. (...) The online resources are great. (...) Well, sometimes it's quicker than the library, like the paper resources.

The flexibility in accessing the library resources greatly benefits the students, as it saves time and effort. Through the LibAccess system, set up by the libraries at McMaster, students can access library resources, including online databases, journals, and library book holdings, from the luxury of their homes.

> On a more daily basis, the resource I use most is the library, especially LibAccess. Well, the health science library... Mostly, it's researching articles, journals, [and] background on whatever. And I usually do that (...) through the health science library or online. That's the number one resource. And I think it's a very powerful resource.

LearnLink: The Little Red Schoolhouse

> LearnLink of course is always important and excellent and we shall forever worship it.

[28][113] Have you ever been "addicted" to the Internet? Or felt passionate about a chat program? Those message forums where you end up reading every post because you just can't help it? Do you think it is something you would spend your time on in university: chatting, reading, writing posts, and surfing the Internet? In the BHSc Program, students have a chance to access these features over LearnLink, an interactive software that allows students and faculty to network in a surprisingly intimate fashion. LearnLink is an important tool for learning, sharing, and communicating. LearnLink has many features, each serving specific functions.

---

[28] As you've just learned, LearnLink was implemented in the 1990s to improve communication between students and faculty. Read on to find out how this program has grown into a cornerstone of the BHSc Program!

[113] How does LearnLink help students in their learning? Read on to find out!

Box 4.2

LearnLink Features and Functions

- Personal Mailbox: This feature allows you to access email and everything else in one place.
- Post Messages: You can read and post messages in every folder to which you have access.
- Folders: The folders can be specific to your courses, some which only certain students can access (like the ones enrolled in the class, course, or program). They can be for messages relating to social events (The Patio), to non-academic concerns (Outside the Classroom), announcements by the Program (BHSc Announcements), etc. You can also request for a personal conference folder for you and your group members to easily share research.
- Instant Message: Using this function, you can chat privately with anyone who is online. You can also save your important conversations.
- Check History: This feature allows you to check if your group members have received your message.
- Calendars: You can use this tool to maintain your own timetable or schedule group meetings.

LearnLink provides a space for the collaborative initiatives of students and faculty members to blossom.[85,79] It is a quick, easy, and comprehensive method of communication. The BHSc students start to use LearnLink in the first year, with the initial encouragement provided by the facilitators. Many students find LearnLink useful in various aspects of their learning, especially for their classes and for exchanging feedback:

> I didn't use LearnLink at all last year in [the general science program] but I find myself spending so much time on LearnLink this year. It's like a very important part. LearnLink is such an amazing program. Whenever I reflect on what kind of program it really is, it's totally amazing because basically you're pretty much kept up to date. [It's] so much better than going to a course website or even a course blog. It's much more efficient and much more useful. (...) You can check your email if anybody wants to have a discussion outside of class. You have your course [folders]. You have [folders for] other forums too: You have the scholarly matrix. You have all the different clubs out there. Basically, everything in health sciences is on LearnLink. So if you're looking for any information, you can just go into their folder and you can find out. Or you

---

[85,79] Usage of LearnLink is one way students are able to build community and collaborate. What are some other approaches towards teamwork and collective learning? Turn to page 85 to explore experiences of working together in classroom settings for BHSc students. LearnLink also provides opportunities where BHSc students can develop rapport to further facilitate communication. How is this culture like? If you are curious, go to page 79.

can just post it. For example, the BHSc private folder on LearnLink, that has a lot of helpful resources too. So if anybody is looking for any help on an assignment, they can just ask you a question. What did you guys get for this question? That kind of thing. So it's much more collaborative. It's much easier to [receive help from] the people that you have around you and it's much easier for you to be useful for them. So LearnLink is an amazing resource.

Students also found that LearnLink benefits their learning through allowing them increased contact with faculty and teaching assistants outside the classroom.

I find that the professors who teach in the [BHSc program] are also very adamant about using LearnLink and they're very open to responding to students' questions. So not only will you receive responses from fellow students, but you might also receive from your professors. And I think that's a huge, huge strength in terms of learning.

In addition to accessing the faculty resources, students also value receiving help from peers or just enjoy talking with them. LearnLink allows students from each year, from different faculties, majors, minors, backgrounds, places, schools, opportunities, and experiences to use each other's help. Through the discussion threads on LearnLink, students have the opportunity to share perspectives, opinions, and ideas on a particular topic that may or may not be academic. LearnLink also functions as a social outlet and a networking tool to foster a sense of community in the BHSc students.

We have LearnLink as a huge tool to talk to people, you know, talk to our whole class really, and post questions, and (...), get answers, and get points of views. (...) I think it's a major part of our culture.

One resource that immediately comes to mind is LearnLink, which is a great tool that helped me not only academically but also socially.

Although LearnLink is found to be an important tool, it was not an immediate discovery for all. Some students found that they had to become accustomed and familiar with LearnLink before they found it useful as a resource:

I have to admit when I came into [BHSc], I was very anti-LearnLink. And it's got this "Nerdlink" moniker that all the [non BHSc students] kids call it. (...) And I guess some of us [in BHSc also] call it Nerdlink. But it really is so convenient. I really love it now. Like my first semester, I used it for about 4 hours [in total] I think. Now I'm at weeks [for total usage]. But it's really convenient. And you get that great interaction. You can ask people for help [and] it's really easy to find people, even people that you don't [see regularly]. [Without LearnLink], in order to interact with them outside of [class], you need to get their contact information and all this e-mail address. Whereas on LearnLink, you just need [their] name [to find them]. (...) I think that it's a great resource. I use it a lot.

At first it was a little overwhelming: so many posts, so many folders. You don't know where you go to find out information. But now I'm used to it and I know where to go if I need chem[istry] help; I can go to the chem[istry] chit-chat folder. Or if you need upper-year help, you can just post in Health Science Students Only [folder].

The importance of LearnLink may be recognized, but the extent of its usage depends upon the prerogative and preference of individual students. Whereas some students are immediately consumed in LearnLink, others use it only because it is necessary.

The main resource used by BHSc students to the greatest degree is LearnLink. This has definitely had some impact on how I communicate with others, organize my schedule and research, and get help. However, I am not one who spends that much time on LearnLink, simply because I consider myself to be less of a "computer person." I am sure that there are some who have LearnLink on consistently throughout the day and check in all the folders regularly, but I use LearnLink when I have to, check up on things from time to time, and use it primarily for its most practical reasons.

LearnLink is not well received by all the students. Some are not pleased with the emphasis placed on using it. For example, most course notes are posted on LearnLink and participation marks are sometimes awarded for discussion, collaboration, and assistance in certain courses. Some students find some of these aspects overwhelming or irrelevant as demonstrated by the following quotes:

I definitely think the amount of emphasis put on LearnLink is too much. I'm computer literate; I can do computers. I'm okay with them, but I just hate how we have to [post in discussion threads] for part of our mark. Sometimes you really just don't feel like posting anything. You might read something and you['re] just sick of it, because some people just write for the sake of writing. So I definitely think LearnLink is a good source for communication even though a lot of people still use MSN [Messenger]. It's definitely a good thing but the amount of emphasis put on it should be reduced.

But sometimes I find that things get repetitive on LearnLink. Like "Are you selling a formal ticket? I'm looking for a formal ticket!" Just read the other posts! (…) But overall it's pretty useful.

Events

The BHSc Program sponsors several events throughout the year. These include pub nights, formals, bowling, class trips, workshops, fashion shows, and many others organized by the various BHSc student committees. These social events give students the chance to meet each other in a non-academic environment and enjoy their time together.

> We have a lot of social events that brings us together all the time, so we get to know each other well. And because we know each other so well, we can work more efficiently with each other [and solve group] problems. (...) I like how in BHSc, we don't compete with each other; I don't see any competitions. I think the reason for that, again, is because we have all the social events. Most of us became friends and because of that, there is no real competition. It definitely enhances [my learning] because by having all the social events run by the faculty or by the students, it's one way for me to relax and forget about my textbooks or journal articles. [It is] an excellent way to (...) stay sane in a stress-free environment.

The social activities are more than mere provisions for entertainment. The sense of community and friendliness exemplified above is helpful in creating the environment of learning. It gives students a chance to relax together. Whether it is the Christmas Party, hosted by the administration, or a pub night, hosted by the student social committee, these are gestures that add up to make a difference in student learning.

Communication skills lab
Various students identified the communication skills lab as a resource which has tremendously enhanced their learning. (To find out more about communication skills please go to page 86)

> The resources made available to me by BHSc have definitely affected my experience at McMaster. For example, my Inquiry class was able to interview standardized patients at the Clinical [Skills] Learning Center in the hospital. This has provided me with an opportunity to improve my Inquiry skills and it has enabled me to experience what it is like to talk to patients in a clinical situation. This opportunity has been priceless to my learning experience. The things I learned about communication using this resource has been something that can never be duplicated by a textbook or by an article in the literature.

Anatomy Lab
Imagine: You walk into a big room. Your senses are not pleased because the smell in the room is not only foreign to you, but also initially unbearable. You manage to overcome the unpleasant smell and glance around to explore the room. You see drawings of human body parts posted on the walls. You see models of the human eye, ears, and bones on your right. The curiosity you experience encourages you to walk further inside. There are human hearts, limbs, and the brain embedded in a box filled with a solution. You then dare to open some of the big and small containers; to your surprise, they contain more human limbs, human pelvises, and other body parts.

No doubt, it is overwhelming at first for some students. However, as time passes by, they learn to overcome their distress. The students learn the concepts of human anatomy in lectures; in the lab, they can explore the make-up of the body and prevalent anomalies deviating from idealistic presentation. The anatomy lab is an arena for students to gain hands-on experience and examine human anatomy by seeing, touching, and feeling.

> One resource in particular that comes to mind is the anatomy lab. It was such an amazing experience to be able to work with the cadavers and learn hands-on in an undergraduate program. This was such a unique opportunity, and I'm glad the BHSc has continued to make it a priority.

You would expect to see such a lab in a medical school. Actually, it *is* the lab that McMaster medical students use. The BHSc students feel privileged to have access to such a learning facility.

> We got to use the whole anatomy lab and we're a second year class. Most of the students in there are in nursing or med students (…) It's amazing!

Many BHSc students may intend to pursue a career in health sciences. The experience of students in the anatomy lab provides them with the chance to rethink or reinforce their future ambitions. A student who initially intended on becoming a physician may realize that the distress they experience upon seeing the human cadavers is not something they would like to do in future whereas another individual may absolutely love the opportunity and may decide to pursue it further.

> Access to the BHSc anatomy lab is a great experience. It allows us to experience something which most of us have never seen before. Also, it helps us move closer in determining what we want to do with our future and whether the path we have chosen is best [for us].

With privilege comes responsibilities; the BHSc students feel compassionate for the people who have donated their bodies. When accessing the anatomy lab, the BHSc students learn to respect and take due care of the human specimens.

As evident from the students' views presented above, most of the BHSc students not only use the offered resources, but also find them beneficial to their learning and growth. However, there are also a few students who do not find these resources to be particularly useful. It is hard to decipher the exact reason as to why such students feel this way. If the student had expanded his or her response to explain the reasons for his or her thinking, it would have been clearer. Since, there was only one student out of many included in reflections and interviews, it is safe to claim that the large majority of BHSc students experienced enhanced learning from the resources provided by the BHSc Program.

Final Thoughts
The resources provided by BHSc are specific to the students in that they

provide an environment that fosters the development of skills, especially those important for the Inquiry process. Allowing students to engage in work and play together, providing them with the knowledge of how to use library resources, and giving them freedom and opportunity for self-discovery, allows students to go the extra mile, step by step.[24,134]

[24,134] If you would like to learn more about the Inquiry process and the skills it builds, turn to page 24. To learn more about the authors' perspective, please proceed to page 134.

Topic 5: Methodology & Our Experience

5.1 Methods

[20] Let us imagine for a minute that you are entering third year in the Bachelor of Health Sciences Program. The Inquiry component of third year requires you to choose an Inquiry course based on your interest. You browse through LearnLink to find out more about the different course offerings this year. The following message captured your attention. [106]

Box 5.1

New Course Open to 3rd and 4th Year Students:
HTH SCI 3E03 The Inquiry Book

IMPORTANT NOTES

This course is open to third and fourth year students. If you are interested in signing up for this course, please sign up in the appropriate 3E03 Sign Up folder. This folder will be posted on September 8th at 12:30pm. Guidelines for signing up for 3E03 are listed at the bottom of this message.

This course is a full year commitment. Students who participate in this course will receive credit in 3E03 and 4D03 (if you are in third year) or 4D03

---

[20] You are here to learn more about our research and writing process. As you read about what we did, revisit Topic 2: Inquiry in the Bachelor of Health Science Program" and think of how our process fits the IREC model. How does our process relate to the structure of other Inquiry courses in the BHSc Program?

[106] Learnlink is an educational tool used extensively in the BHSc Program. It allows for open communication between students, faculty and office staff. To learn more about the effect of Learnlink on students' learning experiences, turn to page 106.

and 4WW3 (if you are in fourth year). So, essentially, this course is a 6-unit commitment.

There will be a brief screening process for this course section that will be talked about on the first day. Course expectations will be outlined during the first class on September 13th. Please LearnLink [the facilitator] or email her at (...) for more information.

Wow, how exciting! A new course is being offered this year. How do you suppose this course will be structured? How would you design it?

Let us continue to read the message.

Box 5.2
The Inquiry Book: Inquiry Course 2005-2006

The Learning Opportunity
Learners who will be interested in this course experience will be those individuals who wish to be involved as principle authors, in a unique qualitative group research project

The "Project"
Assess the activities, attitudes, experiences and learning benefits (if any) of the Inquiry courses; on the BHSc students and curriculum.

The Background Story
As those familiar with the BHSc Program are already aware, Inquiry methods are a central cornerstone in the BHSc curriculum and have transformed the learning environment. Inquiry courses have promoted the ability to identify and solve problems, to think critically, to work in groups and to communicate more effectively.

Students and graduates have acclaimed the positive influence the Inquiry courses have had on the achievement of both their educational and personal goals. This past year, the first year Inquiry facilitators received McMaster Universities' President's Award for Excellence in Teaching and Course Design and the National Educational Award for Collaborative Projects that improve Student Learning. The letters of support from students, the graduates and faculty continue to rise and the time has come, for this legacy to be research, analysed and published.

Our Goal
Within a small learning group, students will employ Inquiry methods and processes to analyze the B. H. Sc. Program Inquiry courses. What better way to demonstrate the process of Inquiry in knowledge acquisition then to have students, instead of faculty, publish the results.

Time Line/Objectives
At this point in time, a group of two (...) are hoping that by April 2006 the course group members will have researched, analyzed and prepared for publication a series of manuscripts/book. *Of course the actual time line will be decided by the group members.*

Course General Information
- This Inquiry course is open to both 3rd and 4th year BHSc Program students.
- Enrolment is limited but flexible. We are committed to keeping the groups small.

- There is an expectation that students will be the principle authors and as such should have advanced writing and research skills. This is an expectation <u>not</u> a requirement.
- Express your interest and ask your questions to [the facilitator] on [LearnLink] (...)

Please feel free to contact me if you have any questions or concerns.

Learning about the effects of Inquiry? Conducting research? Designing your own course and a study project with a group of your peers? Wow, how intriguing! Based on this brief description, you decide to enroll in the Inquiry Book Project. As you enter the classroom on the first day, you meet your peers. Everyone is anxious, nervous and excited about this new course. As members of the class introduce themselves, you realize you will be working with twelve other third year students and two fourth year students on this project for the rest of the year. You feel the excitement in the air!

After the large group introduction and smaller group discussions, your peers come up with many great ideas for this project. There are so many great ideas out there! However, everyone seems overwhelmed and no one knows where to start. The class asks the facilitator if she would help us out. Guess how the facilitator answered us?

Box 5.3
"[Facilitator], we are stuck with this project already. Where should be begin?"

Which one of the following is her reply?

A. Okay, we are doing the research in a specific manner. Please take out your textbook and follow the research protocol.
B. Well then you won't pass the course, will you?
C. Where do you think you should begin?
D. None of the above

Answer: [c]

The first class just ended and you are more puzzled than before the class started. At this point in time, you feel the anxiety and stress which accompanies every Inquiry process at the beginning.[37] You realize you are working with your third and fourth year peers, who have also been through the many stages of Inquiry. This time around, the feelings are tolerable and everyone decides to continue to brainstorm and capture as many ideas as possible for next class.

The first month of school has just passed. Everyone has done a lot of work and there are still many great ideas, but no one knows what to do with them. Problems begin, as the project appears to be going in circles. You and your peers have interviewed research experts, conducted background research, and debated many, many times. The class has come to the realization that no other research of this kind has been done before, which is studying the effects of Inquiry from the students' perspective.

The furthest progress that the class has achieved appears to be coming up with a proposal to compare the BHSc Program, which uses Inquiry, to the other faculties at McMaster which do not use Inquiry. Possible ideas include comparing student marks or student satisfaction on a visual analogue scale, looking at success after graduation, or looking at graduate and professional school acceptance rates. These suggestions seem great at first, but looking at further implications of possible results, you realize the comparisons will not tell the much about the effects on Inquiry. The class has come to the realization that thinking about this project in a very quantitative manner, which is something that you and your peers are comfortably accustomed to, will not yield any insightful or meaningful results.

Wait a minute! Let us backtrack to the class's original objective. Our objective is to tell the effects of Inquiry as a learning method of students' learning. What could be a better way to capture the effects of Inquiry on student learning than to ask the students themselves by conducting a qualitative study? Hak and Maguire (2000) claim that the behaviors which facilitated desired cognitive outcomes of problem-based learning can be explored through qualitative research. (At this point, we realized the original description for the course was to conduct a qualitative study. See Course Description in Box 5.2. How did we miss that one?) Thinking outside of our comfortable and confined quantitative realms, the class explored qualitative research mythologies. Another epiphany was reached at one of the meetings when a member half-jokingly suggests that we go with a *Choose Your Own Adventure* storybook. Perfect! Inquiry is very adventurous to say the least. Using a story-like, pick-your-own-path book to unfold our findings about Inquiry and tell the experiences of BHSc students literally captures the essence of Inquiry.

---

[37] Inquiry in the BHSc Program tends to evoke a range of emotions from students going through various stages of adjustment. You may have experienced similar emotions in new situations such as changing schools or starting a new job. What emotions would you expect to be expressed by students put into a different learning environment than they are used to? To explore this concept further, turn to page 37.

Now that the class has unanimously agreed to focus on qualitative research methods and to present the findings in a *Choose Your Own Adventure* format, everyone is ready to work hard once again and get this project started!

Pilot Study

In studying different qualitative methods, the class has decided to conduct a pilot study using interviews and questionnaires. The purpose of conducting a pilot study was to decide what type of data collection techniques would allow for the most diverse and descriptive data. The pilot study would also allow the researchers to redefine questions according to feedback received from interviewees and analysts. We decided to explore the findings from both structured and ethnographic interviews, as well as through a reflection form.

To organize the pilot study, four students from the class were trained to conduct all of the interviews. A committee of three students was created to study the different types of questionnaires and design the pilot reflection forms. A sub-group of three peers from the class were designated to keep track of the logistics of the pilot study. These logistics include obtaining ethics approval for the pilot study, randomizing potential participants for the study, and scheduling all the interviews and questionnaires. Finally, the remaining committee of four students would analyze all the interviews and questionnaires for common themes and revisions for the actual study.[85,134]

Box 5.4
Structured Interview Questions: Pilot Study   **The Inquiry Experience**
1) What did you expect Inquiry to be like when you entered the program?
2) How satisfied are you with your Inquiry experience?
3) Tell us a story that stands out in your memory about an experience you had in Inquiry?
4) Tell us about any negative experiences you had with Inquiry?
5) (For Upper Years only!) Is there anything else you would like to add with regards to Upper Year Inquiry?
6) How has the Inquiry experience influenced you personally and/or academically?
7) How has your opinion of Inquiry changed over time?
8) Based on your experience in this program, how would you define In-

---

[85,134] A crucial aspect of Inquiry in the BHSc Program is group learning. Students encounter a variety of group projects throughout their education, with groups of many sizes. Do you prefer to work in groups or independently? How do you think students are able to interact cohesively within a group setting to reach a common goal? Delve deeper into students' ideas surrounding group dynamics on page 85. You may also be interested in learning about the authors' group learning experiences on page 134.

quiry?

BHSc Resources
1) What resources does the Bachelor of Health Science program offer you?
2) The next three questions are about BHSc's human resources, physical resources and financial resources and the way that they have influenced you:
   a. Are you satisfied with BHSc human resources?
   b. Are you satisfied with the physical resources?
   c. Are you satisfied with the financial resources?
3) What changes would you make to the resources in BHSc in order to improve your learning and social environment?

4) What resources would you be willing to give up?
5) How do you think the BHSc Program compares to other faculties in terms of the amount of resources it offers?
6) Has your opinion of these resources changed over time?

BHSc Culture
1) What would you say defines the culture of the BHSc Program?
2) What did you expect the BHSc culture to be like before entering the program?
3) In what aspects has this culture affected you?
4) Do you feel that the culture within BHSc has influenced your relationships with other students?
5) Would the BHSc faculty be the same without the culture?
6) How has your opinion of the BHSc culture changed over time?

Facilitators
1) What did you expect from your first year facilitator?
2) Did your first year facilitator meet your expectations, and did this help or hinder your learning?
3) What roles have your facilitators (including Upper Year Facilitators) played in your learning?
4) Were you aware of your facilitator's background? If so, how did this affect your experience?
5) How much contact did you have with your facilitators?
6) Did your opinion of your facilitators change over time?

Myths
1) In your opinion, what do other faculties think of BHSc students?
2) As a BHSc student yourself, what is your personal opinion of the BHSc Program and of the BHSc students?

3)   These opinions that you've talked about, how do they affect you?
4)   What is your personal experience with BHSc students?
5)   As a BHSc student, what is your experience with other faculties?
6)   How have your opinions of BHSc students and of the BHSc Program changed over time?

Box 5.5

Ethnographic Interview: Pilot Study

The Ethnographic interviews were conducted in a dynamic manner between the interviewer and the participant. There were no pre-determined questions, but the same themes served as the basis of this conversational interview style:

The Inquiry Experience

BHSc Resources

BHSc Culture

Facilitators

Myths

Box 5.6[122]

Reflection Form

The following is the reflection form that the class created as a written questionnaire for the pilot study.

1.   a)   What were your expectations of Inquiry when you were coming into the program?
     b)   Describe your general experience with Inquiry.
2.   Tell us a story that stands out in your memory about an experience you had in Inquiry.
3.   a)   What role did the facilitator(s) play in your experience of Inquiry?
     b)   Were you aware of your facilitator's background? Did this influence your learning?
4.   Do you think there is a culture created by BHSc and its students? Please describe this culture, what it means to you, and how it has personally affected you.
5.   Have the resources made available to you by BHSc affected your ex-

---

[122] Here are the reflections questions used in our study!

perience at McMaster? If so, in what ways?
6. What general perceptions do you think other McMaster students have about the BHSc Program, and to what extent are these perceptions accurate? What effects, if any, did it have on your learning?
7. What is Inquiry to you?
8. Is there anything else you wish to tell us?

As for the logistics group, after the pilot study proposal passed ethics approval, the research team obtained a full list of students within the BHSc Program. From this list, the logistics group created a *Microsoft Excel* file of the student names by year in order to stratify randomization according to experience with Inquiry. Using the randomization formula "=RAND()*(b-a)+a" with the respective number of students as variable "b" and 1 as constant "a", the group randomized the pilot study's participant.

After a participant name is randomly selected, an invitation message is sent out. The invitation message explains what the project is about and asks if the individual wishes to participate or not. Below is what the invitation message looks like:

Box 5.6

Invitation Message

Dear _____,

Congratulations! You have been randomly selected to participate in the Inquiry Book Pilot Project. If you have not seen the posts on LearnLink, please see the attached announcement for details of the project.

You now have the choice to accept or decline this invitation. Should you agree to participate you will be randomized into one of two groups: reflection or interview.

If you are in the reflection group, you will be sent a form with a series of questions about Inquiry that we would like you to answer to the best of your ability. You will have one week to fill out this form.

If you are in the interview group, you will be asked to participate in a videotaped interview. More information on the reflections and interviews will be sent to those participants who are randomized to each respective group.

What are the Interviews and Reflections like? Topics addressed in the Interviews and Reflections will include:
- Your personal feelings/accounts of your first year Inquiry experience
- Your experience with courses which utilize the Inquiry format: the triumphs, challenges, struggles, etc.
- Your experiences as a student within the BHSc Program
Please reply to this message by [date]. If you have any concerns at any time,

please feel free to reply to "Inquiry Book Project."
We understand that this project requires some time and effort on your part, but this project will only be successful if the participants are committed.

Thank you in advance,

The Inquiry Book Project↩120

When the randomly selected individuals reply, their responses are recorded. If the response is an unwillingness to participate, then the logistics group randomized and contacted another individual of the corresponding year (first, second, third, or fourth year). If the response is a willingness to participate, then the logistics group uses the randomization formula "=RAND()*(b-a)+a" to allocate this individual into one of three possible groups (structured interview, ethnographic group or reflection questionnaire). Using these *Microsoft Excel* formulas with the corresponding numbers, where the value 3 is the variable "b" and 1 is the constant "a", selection of participants and group allocation are fully randomized.

Box 5.7

A Message to Randomized Interview Participants

Dear _____,

Thank you for your interest in the Inquiry Book Project Pilot study. You have been randomly selected to participate in a taped interview session.
Interviews will be held in the Clinical Learning Centre in the Health Sciences Centre. Interviews will be approximately 45 minutes in length. Interviews will be conducted by two people, one interviewer and one scribe. Please be sure to leave adequate time to participate in your taped interview session.
Please review the available timeslots below and reply to "Inquiry Book Project" with your top five choices for an interview time by [Date]. If your availability is limited to fewer timeslots, please advise us of your situation in your reply. If you miss the deadline, please reply anyway, and we will try to fit you in to a timeslot, but you will have shorter notice of your allotted time.

Monday, [Date]   12:30 - 1:30 pm
                        1:30 - 2:30 pm
                        2:30 - 3:30 pm
                        3:30 - 4:30 pm
                        4:30 - 5:30 pm

↩120 Please jump to page 120 to read the reflection questions.

Tuesday, [Date]	12:30 - 1:30 pm
	1:30 - 2:30 pm
	2:30 - 3:30 pm
	3:30 - 4:30 pm
	4:30 - 5:30 pm
Wednesday, [Date]	8:30 - 9:30 am
	9:30 - 10:30 am
	10:30 - 11:30 am
	11:30am - 12:30 pm
Thursday, [Date]	8:30 - 9:30 am
	9:30 - 10:30 am
	10:30 - 11:30 am
	11:30am - 12:30 pm
	12:30 - 1:30 pm
	1:30 - 2:30 pm
	2:30 - 3:30 pm
	3:30 - 4:30 pm
	4:30 - 5:30 pm

You will receive an additional message detailing the timeslot allotted to you for your taped interview.

Thank you for your continued interest,

The Inquiry Book Project

Box 5.8

A Message to Randomized Reflection Participants

Dear _____,

We would like to begin by thanking you for your participation in our project and taking the time to fill out this reflection form. We assure you that the contents of this form and every aspect of your participation in this project will remain confidential. We ask that you elaborate and share any thoughts or ideas that you feel are relevant when you answer these questions. The accuracy of our research depends on your honesty, so please share all of your views, positive, negative or neutral. You may wish to incorporate the changes in your perspective over time.

Please complete the consent form and fill out the reflection form below and submit it to "Inquiry Book Project" by [Date].

Thank you for your continued interest,

The Inquiry Book Project

Please see below for consent form

Reflection Consent Form

I, _____, as a Bachelor of Health Sciences student randomly selected to participate in the Inquiry Book Qualitative Research Project, understand that the data from this reflection may be used for publication. This data
may include quotations from the reflection that I submit.

I understand that, without further consent, my name, student number, or any
other identifying information will not be used. I give the Inquiry Research team
permission to review the reflection. I understand further that my consent or my
refusal will not be provided to any instructors, the program administration, or
the university. All consent forms will be retained by the Inquiry Book Qualitative Research team.
Any participants wishing to see the results of the research may request to be
notified by the Inquiry Book Qualitative Research team.

I, _____, consent to have my data used for publication purpose.

_____
        Date

The logistics team kept track of all emails sent and received in addition to
the group's Microsoft Excel records file. For confidentiality purposes, names
will not be identified here; however, the number of participants randomized,
willing or unwilling to participate, and group allocation can be displayed.

Box 5.9[131]

Our Records for the Pilot Study.

<u>Random Selection Records</u>

Total Requests Sent | 64 |

Yes | 24 |
No | 11 |
No response | 29 |

<u>Year 1 Random Selection</u>   <u>Year 2 Random Selection</u>

Year 1 INVITATION | 16 | Year 2 INVITATION | 16 |

Year 1 YES | 4 | Year 2 YES | 5 |
Year 1 NO | 3 | Year 2 NO | 3 |
Year 1 NO RESPONSE | 9 | Year 2 NO RESPONSE | 8 |

<u>Year 3 Random Selection</u>   <u>Year 4 Random Selection</u>

Year 3 INVITATION | 16 | Year 4 INVITATION | 16 |

Year 3 YES | 7 | Year 4 YES | 8 |
Year 3 NO | 1 | Year 4 NO | 4 |
Year 3 NO RESPONSE | 8 | Year 4 NO RESPONSE | 4 |

[130]

---

[131] Here are the results of our pilot study!
[130] Please jump to page 130 to see the records for the actual study.

Analysis and Feedback

All pilot interviews were video recorded and transcribed. Transcription included noting everything said and any significant pauses during the interview (Hycner, 1985). The interviews and reflections were then analyzed by a group of four according to a phenomenological approach. This approach allows the authors to investigate the experiences of students without the application of a theory or making any underlying assumptions (Neill, 2004). Each interview was analyzed by all 4 group members in order to identify any themes within each individual interview. In order to avoid biasing beliefs about emotions held by a participant, themes were listed in a positive view and left to data coordinators and writers to decide what quotes best described particular experience. The aim of our research was not to find the "average" experience; instead we wanted to highlight the range of experiences held by individuals within the program. A list of themes was agreed upon by the analyst group and pilot data were re-analyzed by the group with this theme list,

---

Box 5.10
Our Noted Themes

1. Opinions
   a. Familiarity with Inquiry/process
   b. Expectations (of course, of student, of facilitator, etc.)
   c. Important (culture, resources, Inquiry)
2. Emotions
   a. Confusion / Frustration
   b. Satisfaction (dissatisfied/satisfied)
   c. Comfort (nervousness) (in group, with process, with course, adjustment (e.g., to university, fear, confidence)
3. Social interaction/Relationships
   a. Relationships related to academics
   b. Personal relationships / friendships
   c. Diversity of people/ideas
   d. Intrafaculty closeness (or lack of)
   e. Interfaculty closeness (or lack of)
   f. Trust
   g. Support/Help
   h. Collaboration
   i. Group work
   j. Competition (with self/with other)
   k. Conflict (resolution)
4. Skills

---

a. Transferable/practical skill (name skill...)
b. Academic development/improvement (knowledge base)
c. Personal Growth
d. Self evaluation/reflection
e. Feedback
f. Skill development (time management, communication, critical appraisal, etc.)

5. Inquiry
   a. Process/gradual development (learning how to learn)
   b. Self-directed learning
   c. Exploration / flexibility / student empowerment
   d. Structure (or lack of)
   e. Grades (subjective/objective/not important/unsaid importance)
   f. Importance (or not learning anything)
   g. Diversity of experience
   h. Positive OR Negative Experience
   i. Easy

6. Resources
   a. Accessibility (resource)
   b. Quantity (not enough/too much of...)
   c. Quality (poor/excellent/important)
   d. Human/physical/financial (name)
   e. Room for improvement/change (name)

7. Personal characteristics (BHSc students/ facilitators/ peer tutors)
   a. Approachable
   b. Open-mindedness
   c. Maturity
   d. Elitist / Superiority / Arrogant
   e. Friendly
   f. Pride
   g. Involvement (extra-curricular/volunteer/social)
   h. Responsive
   i. Directive (passive/active)
   j. Guidance (personal/course selection)
   k. Intelligence (smart, high grades)
   l. Spoiled/complainers
   m. Envy (envious)
   n. Stereotype (associated with being in health science)
   o. Influence of background
   p. Work ethic (keener/book worm/overachiever)

Upon completion of the pilot interviews and reflections, the analysis group submitted the following feedback for modification of interview and reflection technique and questions.

Box 5.11

A Sample of Our Feedback Notes

Interviews

Format
- Hybrid of ethnographic and structured forms.
- Formatted into 5 sections:
    o 1. Nature of Inquiry
    o 2. Resources
    o 3. BHSc Culture
    o 4. Facilitators
    o 5. Myths
- Each section will have several points that the interviewer should surely address.
- Sections can be addressed in any order based on the interviewee's responses, but it would be helpful to address each section as a whole before moving onto another section.

Interview Points to be Covered
1. Nature of Inquiry (Inquiry Experience)
    a. Effect of Inquiry on personal and academic growth
    b. Personal stories (positive and negative experiences)
    c. Comparison with other teaching methods
    d. Influence of Inquiry on other aspects of your life outside of school
    e. Practicality of curriculum and knowledge you have learned
    f. Definition of Inquiry
    g. Expectations of Inquiry
    h. Satisfaction with Inquiry experience
    i. Skills developed in Inquiry
    j. Preparation from BHSc for post University work
    → May be good to address some of these things at the end of the interview.
2. Resources
    a. What resources exist (physical, human, financial)
    b. Influence of these resources on your learning
    c. Use of the resources
    d. Effectiveness of resources
    e. Comparison of BHSc resources to other faculties
    f. Changes to the resources to improve your learning and social

environment
   g. Importance of the resources
3. BHSc Culture
   a. Aspects that define the BHSc culture
   b. Effect of the culture on learning, academic and personal growth
   c. Expectations of the culture
   d. Influence of culture with respects to your relationships
   e. Effects on BHSc without the culture
   → Could be tied in with the myths sections.
4. Facilitators
   a. Role of facilitators
   b. Expectation of facilitators
   c. Importance of facilitators in your learning
   d. Differences in facilitators and effects of this
   e. Awareness of facilitators skills and training and its importance
   f. Contact with facilitators
5. Myths
   a. What other faculties think of BHSc Program
   b. What other faculties think of BHSc students
   c. Effects of the myths on your learning
   d. Experience with other faculties

Suggestions to Interviewer

- When the interviewer is offering their own stories or opinions, they should try to avoid asking if the interviewee agrees with their story or opinion to avoid directing the response (especially with younger years as they tended to agree more with the interviewers). Try to present both sides of the opinion.
- For example, in addressing a theme about competition:
  - Avoid → "I think BHSc students are the most competitive people at McMaster, what do you think about that?"
  - Suggestion → "I think BHSc students are the most competitive people at McMaster, but I have several friends in the program who strongly disagree and think BHSc students focus more on collaboration. What is your belief?"
- Sometimes simply asking to elaborate on a previous answer provides additional quality information.
- Don't always try to focus complete attention on drawing out negative experiences. Still mention that we are looking for a range of experiences, but over-emphasis on negative experiences may influence the interviewee to say something when it is not necessarily significant.
- Specify how different aspects affect learning (ex. Important to determine not just what resources exist, but if they influence a person's

learning).
- The interview must not necessarily be 45 minutes if all aspects have been addressed.

Reflections
- State at beginning of the form that participants should address answers as to how things affect their learning. Otherwise, the same structure and format should remain.

The agreed upon mixed ethnographic-structured interview approach alongside a reflection questionnaire were then used in the study. The logistics team kept track of all emails sent and received in addition to the group's *Microsoft Excel* records file. For confidentiality purposes, names will not be identified here; however, the number of participants randomized, willing or unwilling to participate, and group allocation can be displayed.
125↘

Box 5.12

Records for Final Study

Random Selection Records

Total Requests Sent | 112 |

Yes | 58 |
No | 11 |
No response | 41 |

125↘ Here are the results of our actual study!

| Year 3 INVITATION | 24 | Year 4 INVITATION | 16 |

Year 3 YES	14	Year 4 YES	15
Year 3 NO	4	Year 4 NO	1
Year 3 NO RESPONSE	4	Year 4 NO RESPONSE	0

The participants who accepted the invitation to the study were then randomized into either the reflection or the interview group.

Stratifying by year, 8 participants were randomized into the reflection and 8 participants were randomized into the interview group. In result, each year of the stratification consisted of the same number of representatives in each group. ↪124

These final interviews and reflections were each analyzed by two members of the analyst group according to the previously agreed upon themes. They were then posted for the group. The data coordinators were asked to pull out any quotes which could relate to emotions, group work, personal development, culture, facilitators, skill development as well as physical and human resources. ↪TC This data was then made available to the writer of each section.

There were errors that we encountered during the study that have served as learning points for future research that we may embark upon. One of these errors resulted in a loss of two interviews after they were conducted. The interviews were conducted without a problem, but when trying to transfer them to computers and save them for analysis and transcription purposes, it was discovered that there was no sound on the tape due to the microphone not working. As such, the interviews could not be used or replaced since it was our own methodological error. We learned a valuable lesson from this error, however: always check that equipment is working properly to avoid the loss of data!

This is the point where the group started to see the results from the seven months worth of effort previously put into the study. The concept of writing a book that once scared us all now just seemed to flow and fit together. We really had demonstrated what Inquiry can truly accomplish. We progressed through an array of emotions, learned new skills that we never thought we could possess. We worked with a large group to make a cohesive final product, and developed our own culture as "The Inquiry Book Team" with the help of our amazing

---

↪124 Please jump to page 124 to see the records for the pilot study.
↪TC These themes and ideas are experienced by students in the BHSc Program and by ourselves. The themes ultimately became topics of our Inquiry Book. To explore any of these topics at this time, please refer to the Table of Contents for page numbers.

facilitator.[46] Luckily for us, several members consistently kept a journal to reflect this process.

5.2 Limitations

In addition to the IREC approach[24], we felt it was necessary to obtain feedback from others and reflect on our own work to identify our limitations. Maudsley (2001) introduces several components of evaluation, and claims that the purpose of evaluation is important to identify. Through exploration of our goals, we will explore our decisions that we made during our own Inquiry process, and look at the possible limitations to our research.

Our Goal

The beginning of our own journey was focused on answering what our goal was, who our audience was, and how we would achieve our objectives. Originally, we had intended on conducting a quantitative evaluation of the Inquiry method in the BHSc Program, and we were looking at drawing comparisons between BHSc and other non-professional undergraduate teaching methodologies. Methods of evaluation could be anything from comparing grades, comparing success rates in evaluation measures (such as the Medical College Admissions Test), and looking at success after graduation. However, we found that these ideas would not truly answer the questions around student experience. But why do we want to know student experience instead of looking at these evaluation measures?

Unlike a professional program where you are able to look at measures on an exam for the professional college, the BHSc Program is a non-professional undergraduate degree, and therefore individuals graduate with diverse experiences and enter a variety of paths. Therefore, it would be extremely difficult to obtain a representative quantitative measure. Looking at final Grade Point Averages (GPAs) would also be fruitless because the courses that BHSc students take have different methods of evaluation and different course content when compared with similar lecture-based courses. Our decision to use a qualitative approach stems from the fact that there were few reliable quantitative methods of evaluation, and it was not our intent to draw comparisons between a lecture-based and Inquiry-based curriculum. We were now left with sampling from the BHSc Program exclusively using a qualitative approach to find out directly from

---

[46] Facilitators are an integral part of the Inquiry experience. You may have had experiences with teachers who dictate information from the front of the room, or you may have had experiences more like the Inquiry approach, where the teacher becomes a learner and part of the group. Which experience do you think you would prefer? To read how students feel about Inquiry facilitators, flip to page 46.

[24] For more information on the Inquiry process, turn to page 24.

students what is important in the program, and what benefits and drawbacks exist from Inquiry.[113]

Limitations of our Study

Once our method for data collection and our goal had been decided, we set out to interview and obtain reflections from BHSc students stratified by year in the program. It is a potential limitation that we did not contact any graduate students for interviews and reflections. It may have added to our data to find out whether or not students continue to feel that Inquiry has helped them with their career or academic endeavours after graduation. However, given that our program is young, the majority of individuals graduating from the program are either in professional school or graduate school. Therefore, graduates are still in the role of students and may not yet have had the experiences to see whether Inquiry is beneficial once full-time studies are completed. It would be advisable to contact students five years from now when some students will have completed full-time studies and determine whether they continue to find Inquiry beneficial.

Considering the individuals that were stratified, there were also limitations based on the timing at which we contacted the students. Given that we were in the middle of the semester (November) when we began contacting individuals for the pilot interviews and reflections, the response rate was slightly lower than expected given that several students were too busy to allocate time for this voluntary project. Beyond this, our response rate from first year students was lower than any other level. This was controlled for with the stratification procedure to ensure we had balanced participation from each year; however, several students may have declined participating because of the emotional feelings they were experiencing surrounding the Inquiry process.[37,134] It is possible that we obtained the more positive viewpoints of first year students. This is further amplified considering that most students and facilitators believe that the first two months of the term (September and October) are the times at which the most negative emotions are visible in first year students with the introduction of Inquiry. We may have missed some very rich data by not interviewing during this period.

Data collection involved a 45-minute interview or a short reflection (usually completed in less than four pages). Given the amount of data collected from each individual, the short length of the interview and reflection may have hindered our ability to obtain opinions and bring out truly reflective thoughts. First,

---

[113] For further exploration about our Methodology, turn on page 113.

[37,134] Learning in the Inquiry setting requires many students to move away from their comfort zone of didactic teaching to a more dynamic approach of group learning. Naturally, such an adjustment comes more easily for some students than others. How would you feel to suddenly be working or learning in a foreign environment? To explore how students feel throughout their Inquiry experiences, flip to page 37. Alternatively, to learn about the authors' personal emotional journey and thoughts, jump ahead to page 134.

given that all students were aware that the authors were BHSc students, there is the chance that participants may have felt the need to respond in a certain way or use terminology commonly used within the program. As evident by our research there are some beliefs that are fairly consistent within the student population, and the knowledge that their opinions were being shared with other students may have influenced how honestly the participants responded. We also recognize that there are limitations to reflection (either verbal or written) as a means to capture experience. For example, some participants may not feel comfortable reflecting in front of a camera and to a fellow peer. Other students may require an extended period of time to truly consider how they feel, and therefore experience may not be accurately picked up in a short interview or reflection. This second point is extremely important when considering how long each interview was conducted for. We chose an ethnographic interview style to retrieve information about student experience in a comfortable, reciprocal relationship (Westby, Burda, & Mehta, 2005). With only 45 minutes to conduct an interview, it can be difficult to develop such a relationship. The result is that the quantity of information from a variety of sources may outweigh the depth of information that could have been obtained from conducting a very limited number of interviews for a longer period or over several weeks. The latter would have been more of a case study approach to obtaining student experience and may have resulted in a population that was not representative.

With regards to the data that was obtained, we recognize that the point of our data is not to tell the reader what every student will, on average, experience. We recognize that there is a wide range of experience, and therefore we selected several quotes that highlight the diversity of experiences and emotions students may have, instead of just picking one that would best describe the average student experience. Depending on your goals in reading this book, we may not answer what every student will experience. However, it was our intent to instead highlight that Inquiry is not necessarily predictable, and what each student obtains or experiences through the process may vary greatly between individuals.

We also identified that we did not explore each individual student goals as deeply as we could have. Our original intent was to research specifically on what experiences existed within Inquiry, and although future goals were mentioned in several interviews, these objectives were typically not the focus of the interview for either the participant or interviewer. Upon reflection and receiving feedback from others, we have realized that these goals are a large issue that could be explored further. Several students within the program have goals, such as attending medical school, and these ambitions greatly influence what skills and knowledge are developed, what culture is fostered within the program, and what motivations exist. Further research into career aspirations may elaborate on why we obtained the experiences that we did from the BHSc students.

[112,118] 5.3 Our Group Process

Dear learners,

As your choose-your-own adventure comes to a close, you may be experiencing some sadness, some anxiety, or some closure. Whatever your feelings are, you are now officially an individual who has been enlightened or frustrated (or both!) by the inklings of what constitutes the Inquiry process. Like students in their first year of the Bachelor of Health Sciences program, you explored what it means to work in a group, what it takes to collaborate and communicate, and what it is all about to evaluate, reflect, assess, and construct. One must seek first before they will find; dear learner, you have done just that!

In seeking, the Inquiry Book investigation team also found what we were looking for: our presentation of the students' Inquiry stories in its most authentic, close-to-heart form. Like your adventure, the process in developing this book was wrought with emotions and uncertainty; only ours was assessed within ourselves and with 14 other peers/researchers.

At the end of the project, through written reflections, we shared with each other our insights, feelings, thoughts and interpretations of the Inquiry Book Project. Through our reflections, we hoped to sort out our emotions and gain clarity in the underlying observations of Inquiry that we wish to communicate to our peers. Writing our reflections also assisted us examine our own progress as learners, so that the process of our group work in the future can be improved. With this in mind, we will now share our most inner thoughts and assessment of our Inquiry experiences.

Work and Play

These two distinctive elements define life, but are often so intertwined they may be difficult to separate in practice. For the Inquiry Book team, we were on numerous occasions unable to detach personal feelings from our efforts and contributions in producing this book. As one of our research team members eloquently stated:

> The experiences working within a group of people, for me, are tied to the relationships that I have with my classmates and the experiences that we [shared] this past year. Thus, reflecting upon this particular experience working on the Inquiry book is even more difficult, as it is hard to separate the emotions that [result from our] personal relationships (…).

To effectively provide and receive constructive feedback, suggestions, and even criticisms in this entire process, it was vital that bias and preconceptions based on our friendships with each other be reduced as much as possible. Evidently, it became increasingly challenging as our relations with each other deep-

---

[112,118] How was our Inquiry process? Read on to explore the nature of our Inquiry journey, which we embarked upon to write this book.

ened throughout the year. Typical in any group work, work and play must be separated so that individual contributions are genuinely evaluated with an open mindset on the receiving end. Otherwise, it may lead to the deterioration of group dynamics, discomfort between group members, and overall increased misunderstandings in communication and interactions. Captured in one reflection passage:

> It was frustrating or heartbreaking for me to see some members not being open to being more neutral. It is not an easy thing to do, especially with [so] many different perspectives and pressures on the project at hand. But just standing one step back to see the greater picture in a neutral, objective manner [helps] facilitate the group to be productive.

With this recurring observation, our Inquiry group realized the essential requirement to remain emotionally objective so that team processes would be more effective and efficient.

I can't take it anymore!
[40] Core to the Inquiry process are the feelings of frustration, fear, anxiety, and uncertainty. Imagine yourself walking into a dark forest at twilight hours trying to figure a way out! It certainly was not easy in our journey to hack down all the emotional barriers and scheduling conflicts to ensure that our product would be slowly but surely achieved. Candidly conveyed by one team member:

> Much of this decision-making process was frustrating: I felt like during a lot of these early meetings, we were going around in circles without accomplishing anything substantial.

Another peer researcher expressed:

> Following [our] discussions, I would feel as though we got a lot accomplished, but at the end of the day when I sat down to write my reflection of our class time, I would not be able to come up with one decision we made or agreed upon. For me, this resulted in more anxiety and frustration. I felt that all the work I was putting into the project was a waste since the group would not use it or forget we even discussed it at our next meeting.

Evidently, much of the discussions, especially in the earlier stages of our writing and decision-making steps, were exhaustive but inefficient. However, this was also an integral aspect of Inquiry, hitting roadblocks and learning how to work around them before further progression is made. As much as the emotional toll seemed overwhelming at times, it was also a necessary part of our

---

[40] You have just learned about how frustration in the context of the emotional journey of Inquiry. This section will explain how frustration was a part of the Inquiry Storybook project.

group learning. Confusion and emotional strain was not something new in the Inquiry environment, and we had to learn to deal with such barriers in our group before being able to move forward. By learning how to identify the sources which feed into these complex and sometimes contradictory feelings, our investigation team could better prioritize tasks and categorize our concerns into more organized domains for discussion. As demonstrated in one reflection:

> I was overwhelmed, and I was also worried that none of my peers in the class knew where to start. The only comfortable part was that I knew we were in this together, and we could tolerate these confusing early stages of the Inquiry [process] based on our [previous] courses. And this is how I think our group started to develop, and grew a strong dynamic that helped us manage and deal with many obstacles and external barriers throughout our process.

Say what?

The importance of communication cannot be overemphasized in any group or Inquiry process. For our investigation team, the need to find consensus amongst all 14 of us (plus a facilitator!) was an extremely arduous task. With each of us bringing to the table different concepts and preferences, compounded by our diverse backgrounds and personalities, it is all too imaginable how pressing was the need to be clear in expression and truthful with emotions. Even if it meant that we needed to engage in a painfully long meeting or workshop, so be it (which we did end up doing on many occasions). This way, our reactions to various situations, as well as any brilliant ideas generated by any individual, would be openly shared with everyone for critical analysis, appreciation, or revision. Expressed by one group member:

> Sometimes, I know I can be very focused on the product and what is being "accomplished" (in terms of things physically being done). While this is an important focus, I have learned that it is important to not forget that problem-solving with group members through oft long-winded discussions, formally addressing group conflicts, and planning is just as important as directly working on a product.

It is inevitable that when working in a group, we feel that our individual ideas seem more effective and feasible than those of others. While the implementation of some of these concepts can lead to greater productivity, they must also be first brought out to the entire group so that everyone is supportive of the new course of action. Through having everyone on the same page, the team will be able to mobilize as one unit so that the process is more homogeneous and harmonious.

As well, in any group setting, there may be issues with work ethics and individual contributions that may disrupt positive group dynamics. Thus, it is imperative that all the emotions and related issues be addressed to everyone so that amendments can be made. Certainly, it would not be effective at all to finger-point while the issue at hand remains unresolved, perhaps even unknown to different group members. Stated in one reflection:

> Trusting and being accountable [while] working in a group [is a very important element]; taking this theme into consideration can help ease group conflicts. What I learned is that when a group conflict or when tensions between individuals occur, the issues really need to be addressed openly. One cannot expect an issue to resolve itself by talking about an individual behind his/her back. One can expect the issue to be resolved by taking positive action in trying to address the individual and have an honest, open discussion. Setting up subgroups against another individual (or another subgroup) would do nothing to solve the problem.

Go get them, Tiger!

Working in a large group naturally has its advantages. Especially in good moments, the process is akin to the exciting ascent of a roller coaster ride, with its breathtaking view of what is yet to come, compounded by the exhilaration of the journey itself. In all the fervor and excitement, it is also crucial that the vision for the outcome is feasible, manageable to plan and manageable to execute. As full-time students registered in an undergraduate program, there is a need to set realistic workloads that are achievable in the context of other academic responsibilities. While it is thrilling to believe that we can devote our entire time to such a monumental task of writing the Inquiry Storybook, we also hold duties to other obligations. As one of our group members wisely realized:

> I have learned that I bite off more than I can chew, and I refuse to admit it to myself until it is too late; it is personal goals and initiatives that suffer [as] I look out for others in the group first. I must learn to be more efficient in managing my time, and to be honest with myself and others when I simply cannot take on more work at a particular point in time.

In another reflection:

> In our Inquiry Book Project, we often set many ideal goals that we would get a lot of things accomplished within a very short amount of time. I often do this myself, and end up not sleeping or sleeping very little to get the promised task done. I think this is just a matter of truly taking a minute to evaluate how much time realistically a task would take and take other priorities (as simple as sleeping, showering, or eating) into consideration. We often overexert ourselves by not setting a realistic timeline. A method I have learned is to simply pose the question, "Is this a realistic timeline?" Just being aware of it makes a difference in the planning process.

By seeing in perspective the work that needs to be done, our focus on what could not be completed within a set timeframe becomes a positive impetus for us to determine alternative arrangements. Rather than feeling guilty or disappointed in oneself, or having these feelings projected to the group, an initial, realistic organization of priorities would prevent future setbacks and internal group conflicts. In identifying an absolute commitment to timelines gone astray, one reflection expressed:

> Soon, I understood the Inquiry Book project as a pragmatic operation, and before long, I was proposing rigid agendas and strict meeting formalities. In my eyes, the Inquiry Book team was in desperate need of discipline. We needed to produce, we needed to be practical, and I was ready to attack anything ... and anyone who conflicted with my vision of pragmatism.

One can see how striving for the unmanageable can transform into disaster. It is one thing to be disciplined, but another altogether to understand that we all lead diverse lives beyond our role as writers of the Inquiry Storybook. By seeing the large task at hand with sensitivity, group dynamics would subsequently improve as individuals encountered less of the uncontrollable time constraints and possible chastising by the group.

On the count of three, give me your hand!

Trust. Such a simple word, yet so challenging for our investigation team to comprehend and fully practice. Evidently, this was a naturally difficult element to achieve because all fourteen of us possessed different skills, preferences, insights and learning styles.

While we were each designated various tasks throughout the year, the extent of trust for the completion of these items was not always strong in our process. Particularly when the Inquiry Project was conflicted by other academic obligations, there was great skepticism as to whether tasks would really be completed with highest quality and effort by the designated individual. In one reflection, it was noted:

> Trusting other group members is a very important element in group work. In the beginning of the year, everyone seemed to have a trust and everyone was self-accountable for their work. However, as the workload got heavier, some of this trust disappeared and many minor group tensions resulted. Perhaps one contributing factor is that some members did work behind the scenes. I knew for fact that another member and I did a lot of planning and work behind the scenes regarding the logistics of the pilot study and actual research. My reasoning for not showing every detail of our work is that it would have unnecessarily filled the group folder, especially when tons of other work was being done.

Without a doubt, trust for each other ensued in a sense of responsibility that collated the collective goals of the group. With duty came accountability of the individual so that this bond would be continually preserved. This was described in one reflection:

I have learned the importance of group dynamics and team building. You cannot work in a group without knowing the members of your group and trusting them to complete their tasks effectively and on time.

Ultimately, trust also led to better group dynamics, as communication became open and explicit. In the spirit of our qualitative analysis, understanding how others work and trusting that judgment is vital because we are also the participants of Inquiry. Knowing our peers will fulfill their tasks and speak up if they are unable to (with justified reasons of course!) keeps both work and social relationships healthy and strong.

I think, therefore I am

Despite the continued acknowledgement and understanding that reflections are a core component of the Inquiry process, one of the weaknesses in our investigation team is the lack of transferring thoughts onto paper. As such, it greatly hindered our group development in effectively realizing what worked and what did not. While it became evident in later group discussions that all of us had internalized the events and proceedings of the Inquiry Book Project, there were inconsistencies in terms of bringing these observations and analysis to written form. Expressed by one peer:

> One thing I can carry with me as concrete learning from this process is the importance of reflection. Not only of the importance of personal reflection, but also sharing your ideas of the progress and troubles of a group within the group.

More succinctly described by another team member:

> One of the major struggles that resulted from our group process, I believe, is our lack of ability to effectively reflect upon and assess the group process itself. We had initially set out to record our small group learning in a log, but this was not completed throughout the year. As a result, we do not have an effective mechanism to gauge our learning throughout the year. We did, however, often discuss our learning goals in the large group setting, but documenting this over the year could have provided more appropriate evaluation.

In reflecting, both cognitively and in written communications, individuals within a group and the team as a unit can more concretely specify issues surrounding the processes of the project. Consistently executing the exercise of reflections will also ameliorate communications within the group so that ideas are better critically analyzed. As stated earlier, written reflections can serve to evaluate group processes; how it can be standardized is then dependent on a comparison of the outcomes before and after. In the following excerpt, you will be able to see the lessons gained from our Inquiry Project experience:

I gained another exemplary learning experience through another challenge we faced in this process, involving self and group evaluation. Although I believe I reflected at key points in the process, I did not share my reflections towards the end of the year. This does not affect my individual evaluation of my learning and process. It does hinder our group learning if my peers cannot witness my learning and learn from it. Thus, in my future Inquiry journeys, I will be sure to share my learning and take part in the learning of my peers.

Learning to admit and amend

Inevitably, there were various barriers and challenges encountered by the investigation team this year (which will hopefully lead you, dear learner, to treasure this product you are holding in your hands now even more!). Working in a group of 14 truthfully is a monumental task in itself, save the efforts to continually reflect and assess the process while remaining most neutral and objective to suggested changes, feedback and constructive criticisms. As difficult as the journey is, involving exhaustive discussions, writing workshops, and a demanding workload, it should not be a 'blame and shame' game. While it was easy for anyone in the large group to point fingers and chastise particular individuals, it would be much more effective and healthy for group dynamics to explore the issues at hand. Drastic, positive differences resulted when team members learned to admit that they were unable to finish their allocated task, or were unable to meet an objective, because there was no deception. Expressed in one reflection:

> I knew I was doing my share (and more) of the group's effort, but I was uncertain if other members were doing their share. This curiosity escalated when other members approached me and discussed our concerns for some other members' work ethics. In a way, it is often inevitable that some members contribute more than others. What I learned through some of our group tensions and resolution is that we need to trust other group members; and whenever there is that doubt, we need to approach it and address the issues immediately.

We developed as a group when we realized the importance of being accountable, whether this means a task is complete or not. Without understanding the significance of accountability, the circle of trust will break, as had ours during varying points in our Inquiry process when tensions were also at maximal points.

When the Inquiry Storybook team was able to admit to setbacks caused by negligence, it clarified even further what was most pertinent, in our limited time, to present all the material in the envisioned format. What is this trying to say? Does it flow with the next point? For instance, there was resounding support, later realized in practice, of the benefits and strengths of working in small groups. As one team member attests:

> One of the biggest things I think that I have learned from the group is how important it is to work in small and manageable sized groups. We decided to allow

small groups to have the authority to make decisions on behalf on the entire group and this is something that I will take with me in future group learning projects. It is important to develop an appropriate level of trust amongst group members and once this is achieved, allowing smaller groups to larger scale decisions created effective and efficient results.

By identifying where gaps lay, rather than directing solely and viciously our efforts to blame those who were responsible for them, our team was able to better generate resolutions for productive changes to instead occur.

In Closing...

Coming together is a beginning.
Keeping together is progress.
Working together is success.
-    Henry Ford

It is a moment in time that brings this investigation team together, with all its similarities and differences in personalities, learning styles, and intellect. Every group is different, and this one is no exception. In creating a book to share the stories of Inquiry students, we also share with you our mini-versions of how Inquiry has intertwined and impacted our lives, with all its lessons.

It might be a bit of a stretch to say that Inquiry has been life altering. It certainly is [true] though that all the processes contributing to this book reflected a highly complex and unique amalgamation of circumstances, some predictable, some not. Through it all, what I have learned is that group dynamics is a fascinating thing; it can work extremely well one minute and then disintegrate in the next. With trust, respect, and understanding to others, and commitment, discipline and critical thinking towards yourself, surely the likelihood of success, both as an individual and as a group, will be attainable and most rewarding.

Benchmarking–Part II

After reading this investigation of Inquiry, you may have experienced some of the ins and outs and ups and downs of Inquiry. You may have felt confusion, frustration, comfort and support; all of which have led to your understanding of Inquiry. In order to complete the Inquiry adventure, please complete the benchmarking exercise again and reflect on your learning and progress.
Benchmarking Exercise

Benchmarking Exercise

Please take a moment to answer the following questions:

1. What makes an educated person?

2. What is learning?

3. How do you learn?

4. If you had to ask one scholarly question, what would it be?

5. How would you find an answer(s) to the question you asked above?

Take a look at your first benchmarking exercise and reflect on your Inquiry adventure (see page 2). Did you make progress? Did you learn anything about your strengths and weaknesses? Was anything particularly helpful or unhelpful?

Now you can decide what steps to take to further enhance your understanding of Inquiry.

Bibliography

Arizpe, E., & Styles, M. (2004). Love to learn your book: Children's experience of text in the eighteenth century. History of Education, 33(3), 337-352. Retrieved January 14, 2006, from ERIC database.

Bachelor of Health Sciences. (2005a). About the program: Strengths. Retrieved January 15, 2006, from McMaster University, Bachelor of Health Sciences web site: www.fhs.mcmaster.ca/bhsc/about/strengths.htm

Bachelor of Health Sciences. (2005b). Inquiry: What is Inquiry? Retrieved January 5, 2005, from McMaster University, Bachelor of Health Sciences website: www.fhs.mcmaster.ca/bhsc/Inquiry/Inquirywhat.htm

Banning, M. (2005). Approaches to teaching: Current opinions and related research. Nurse Education Today, 25(7), 502-508. Retrieved January 17, 2006, from CINAHL database.

Bara, J. (2005). Seeds of mistrust: Tribal and colonial perspectives on education in Chhotanagpur, 1834-c. 1850. History of Education, 34(6), 617-637. Retrieved January 14, 2006, from ERIC database.

Barr, R., & Tagg, J. (1995). From teaching to learning–a new paradigm for undergraduate education. Change, 27(6), 12-25. Retrieved January 14 2006, from ERIC database.

Barr, R., Doberneck, D., Fear, F., Petrulis, R., Robinson, C., Smith, J., et al. (2003). Meaning, making and "The Learning Paradigm": A provocative idea in practice. Innovative Higher Education, 27(3), 151-168. Retrieved January 9, 2006, from ERIC database.

Bolhuis, S. (2003). Towards process-oriented teaching for self-directed lifelong learning: A multidimensional perspective. Learning and Instruction, 13(3), 327-347. Retrieved January 14, 2006, from ERIC database.

Brookfield, S.D. (1993). Self-directed learning, political clarity and the critical practice of adult education. Adult Education Quarterly, 43(4), 227-242.Retrieved January 22, 2006, from ERIC database. http://www.nl.edu/academics/cas/ace/facultypapers/ StephenBrookfiel_ Learning.cfm

Brookfield, S.D. (2000, January 2-4). Contesting criticality: Epistemological and practical contradictions in critical reflection. Paper presented at the 40th Adult Education Research Conference. Abstract retrieved January 29, 2006, from http://www.edst.educ.ubc.ca/aerc/2000/brookfields1-web.htm

Brown, J.S., Collins, A., & Duguid, P. (1989). Situated cognition and the culture of learning. Educational Researcher, 18(1), 32-42. Retrieved January 9, 2006, from ERIC database.

Burke, V., Jones, I., & Doherty, M. (2005). Analysing student perceptions of transferable skills via undergraduate degree programmes. Active Learning in Higher Education, 6(2): 132-144.

Canadian Institute of Health Research. (2004). About CIHR. Retrieved January 25, 2006, from http://www.cihr-irsc.gc.ca/e/24418.html

Candy, P.C. (2000). Reaffirming a proud tradition. Active Learning in Higher Education, 1(2): 101-125.

Castles, J. (2004). Persistence and the adult learner: Factors affecting persistencein open university students. Active Learning in Higher Education, 5(2), 166-179. Retrieved January 9, 2006, from ERIC database

Cicchino, P. M. (2001). Love and the Socratic method. American University Law Review, 50, 533-550. Retrieved April 15, 2006 from http://www.wcl.american.edu/journal/lawrev/50/cicchinosocratic.pdf? d=1

Deboer, G. E. (2002). Student-centered teaching in a standards-based world: Finding a sensible balance. Science & Education, 11(4), 405-417. Retrieved April 20, 2006, from PUBMED database.

Dewey, J. (1897). My pedagogic creed. The School Journal, LIV(3), 77-80. Retrieved April 15, 2006, From: http://www.infed.org/archives/e-texts/e-dew-pc.htm

Dewey, J. (1916) Democracy and education: An introduction to the philosophy of education. New York: Free Press. Retrieved May 14, 2006, fromhttp://www.ilt.columbia.edu/Publications/dewey.html

Doig, K., & Werner, E. (2000). The marriage of a traditional lecture-based curriculum and problem-based learning: Are the offspring vigorous? Medical Teacher, 22(2), 173-178. Retrieved January 16, 2006, from ERIC database.

Eisner, E. (1969). Instructional and expressive objectives. In D. Hamilton, D. Jenkins, C. King, B. MacDonald & M. Parlett (Eds.), Beyond the numbers game: A reader in education evaluation. London: Macmillan.

Falvey, L.J. (1996). Learning natural resource principles. In Agricultural education in natural resource management (chap. 9). Retrieved February 5, 2006, from http://www.landfood.unimelb.edu.au/dean/falveybk/ch9.html

Fincher, C. (1991). Tides and trends in higher education. Retrieved January 25, 2006, from ERIC database.

Fisher, R., & Craik, F.I.M. (1977). The interaction between encoding and retrieval operations in cued recall. Journal of Experimental Psychology: Human Learning and Memory, 3(6), 701-711. Retrieved February 3, 2006, from PsycINFO database.

Gentle, P. (2001). Course cultures and learning organizations. Active Learning in Higher Education, 2(1), 8-30. Retrieved January 21, 2006, from PsycINFO database.

Gibbs, G. & Coffey, M. (2004). The impact of training of university teachers on heir teaching skills, their approach to teaching and the approach to learning of their students. Active Learning in Higher Education, 5(1): 87-100. Retrieved January 25, 2006, from ERIC database.

Gray, A. (1997). The road to knowledge is always under construction: A life history journey to constructivist teaching. Unpublished Master's Thesis, University of Saskatchewan, Regina, Saskatchewan, Canada. Retrieved February 6, 2006 from http://www.ssta.sk.ca/research /instruction/97-07.htm

Haddon. (2004). The curious incident of the dog in the night-time. Vintage Books.

Hak, T., & Maguire, P. (2000). Group process: The black box of studies on problem-based learning. Academic Medicine, 75, 769-772. Retrieved October 3, 2005, from CINAHL database.

Harnish, D.H., Barrett, S., Butler, J., Cates, E., deLottinville, C., Jordana, M., et al. (2005, January). [Skill Development with Students and Explicit Integration Across Four Years of the Curriculum.] Project submitted for the 2005 Alan Blizzard Award, as part of the 25th Annual Society for Teaching and Learning in Higher Education Conference, Charlottetown, Prince Edward Island, Canada.

Haskins, C. H. (1923). The rise of universities. New York: Henry Holt. Retrieved April 24, 2006, from http://www.questia.com /PM.qst?a=o&d=814563

Henderson, N.K. (1969). The nature of universities. University Teaching. New York, NY: Dell Publishing.

Huitt, W. (2001). Humanism and open education. Educational Psychology Interactive. Retrieved February 5, 2006, from Valdosta State University, Educational Psychology Department Web site: http://chiron.valdosta.edu/whuitt/col/affsys/humed.html

Hychner, R.H. (1985). Some guidelines for the phenomenological analysis of interview data. Human Studies, 8(3), 279-303. Retrieved October 13, 2005, from E-Journals @ McMaster database.

Johnson, D. W., Johnson, R. T. (1999). Making cooperative learning work. Theory into Practice, 38(2), 67-73. Retrieved February 24, 2006, from ERIC database.

Julian, E. R. (2005). Validity of the Medical College Admission Test for predicting medical school performance. Academic Medicine, 80(10), 910-917. Retrieved April 14, 2006, from EMBASE database.

Kohn, A. (2004). What does it mean to be well educated? Boston, MA: Beacon Press.

Lomas, L. (1997). The decline of liberal education and the emergence of a newmodel education and training. Education & Training, 39(3), 111-115. Retrieved January 16, 2006, from E-journals - Scholars Portal database.

Levett-Jones, T. L. (2005). Self-directed learning: Implications and limitations for undergraduate nursing education. Nurse Education Today, 25(5), 363-368. Retrieved December 12, 2005, from CINAHL database.

MacDonald, P. (1991). Selection of health problems for a problem-based curriculum. In D. Boud & G. Felleti (Eds.), The challenge of problem based learning (pp. 101-110). London: Kogan Page.

Maudsley, G. (2001). What issues are raised by evaluating problem-based undergraduate medical curricula? Making healthy connections across the literature. Journal of Evaluation in Clinical Practise, 7(3), 311-324. Retrieved May 2, 2006, from EMBASE database.

McAlpine, L. (2004). Designing learning as well as teaching: A research-based model for instruction that emphasizes learner practice. Active Learning in Higher Education, 5(2), 119-134. Retrieved February 19, 2006, from ERIC database.

Mutch, A. (2003). Exploring the practice of feedback to students. Active learning in Higher Education, 4(1): 24-38.

Neill, J. (2004). Analysis of professional literature: Qualitative research. Retrieved September 23, 2005, from http://www.wilderdom.com/research/QualitativeVersusQuantitativeRes earch.html

Norman, G.R. (1999). The adult learner: A mythical species. Academic Medicine, 74(8), 886-889.

Owens, L.D., & Walden D.J. (2001) Peer instruction in the learning laboratory: A strategy to decrease student anxiety. Journal of Nursing Education, 40 (8) 375- 377. Retrieved Feburary 23, 2006, from ProQuest Nursing Journals database.

Ozuah, P.O. (2005). First, there was pedagogy and then came andragogy. The Einstein Journal of Biology and Medicine, 21, 83-87. Retrieved

January 6, 2006, from http:// www.aecom .yu.edu/home/ejbm /PDFs / Volume _ 21/Number_2/21Ozuah83.pdf

Pithers, R.T. (2000). Critical thinking in education: A review. Educational Research, 42(3), 237-249. Retrieved January 19, 2006, from ERIC database.

Postman, N., Weingartner, C. (1969). Teaching as a subversive activity (pp. 25-38) New York, NY: Dell Publishing.

Railton, D. & Watson, P. (2005). Teaching autonomy. Active Learning in Higher Education, 6(3): 182-193.

Rangachari, P. K. (1991). Design of a problem-based undergraduate course in pharmacology: Implications for the teaching of physiology. American Journal of Physiology 6(3), S14 S21. Retrieved April 20, 2006, from PUBMED database.

Rangachari, P. K. (2004). Caring for students: A teacher's view. Biochemistry and Molecular Biology Education, 32(1), 3-6. Retrieved April 20, 2006, from PUBMED database.

Rosovsky, H. (2005). Evaluation and the Academy: Are we doing the right thing? Retrieved April 23, 2006, from American Academy of Arts and Sciences web site: http://www.amacad.org/publications/rosovsky.aspx

Simonelli, R. (1996). Partnering with indigenous education. On Common Ground, 7, 23-25. Retrieved December 29, 2005, from http ://www.yale .edu /ynhti/pubs/A20/simonelli.html

Thorpe, M. (2000). Encouraging students to reflect as part of the assignment process: Student responses and tutor feedback. Active Learning in Higher Education, 1: 79-92.

Topping K. J. (2005) Trends in Peer Learning. Educational Psychology, 25 (6) 631-645. Retrieved Feburary 23, 2006 from Taylor & Francis Group database.

Uljens, M. (2001). On General Education as a Discipline. Studies in Philosophy and Education, 20(4), 291-301. Retrieved January 16, 2006, from ERIC database.

Vanderstraeten, R., & Biesta, G.J.J. (2001). How is education possible? Preliminary investigations for a theory of education. Educational Philosophy and Theory, 33(1), 7-21. Retrieved January 14, 2006, from Taylor & Francis Group database.

Vaughn, L. M., Baker, R. C., DeWitt, T. G. (2000). The adult learner: A misinterpreted species? Academic Medicine, 75(3), 215-216. Retrieved April 14, 2006, from EMBASE database.

Westby, C., Burda, A. N. & Mehta, Z. (2005). Asking the right questions in the right ways: Strategies for ethnographic interviewing. Retrieved May 3, 2006, from http://www .asha.org/ about /publications /leaderonline/ archives /2003/ q2/f030429b.htm

Zeszotarski, P. (1999). New Dimensions of the Community College Curriculum
    (Report No.JC990-092). Los Angeles, California: University of
    California. (ERIC Document Reproduction Service No.ED427797)
Zimmerman,B., Lindberg,C., & Plsek,P. (1998). Edgeware: Insights from
    complexity science for health care leaders.

Index

About the Authors

Our team consists of fourteen senior level students from the Bachelor of Health Sciences (Honours) Program at McMaster University (Hamilton, Ontario, Canada). Over the past few years, we have used the process of Inquiry to guide our learning. As a group, we felt that it would be valuable to examine Inquiry within the Program and educate others on this method of learning. In keeping with the spirit of Inquiry, this project was undertaken using the process and principles of Inquiry.

What Inquiry Means To Us

"Inquiry is the process of becoming human"
- *Randy Ai*

"For me, Inquiry is a paradox. I must take control and yet never have control of my learning. This is a good thing."
- *Dr. Sheila Barrett, facilitator*

"Inquiry is the process of inquiring how to inquire, or in other words learning how to learn. For me, Inquiry has fostered the development and application of skills such as critical thinking, research, communication, and collaboration towards accomplishing learning objectives in subject areas ranging from biochemistry to educational research."
- *Mihir Bhatt*

"Inquiry is the process of developing skills and applying them to lifelong learning. Inquiry has allowed me to self-evaluate and improve upon my weaknesses."
- *Stephanie Chevrier*

"For me, Inquiry is something that has allowed me to expand my world view. It is something that has given me the confidence to do what I want to do."
- *Robert Ciccarelli*

"Inquiry is learning without fences, boundaries and rules. It's like riding a wild horse. It can be scary, exciting, exhilarating but sometimes painful. You're never in control and that's the beauty of it."
- *Rosheen Grady*

"Inquiry has become a way of life for me. It has presented me with life-changing learning experiences and unforgettable lessons, many of which I taught to myself."
- *Vandana Kumari*

"Inquiry is all about taking control of your learning, your education. It is student-driven and student-oriented, and you literally get back what you put in."
- *Kayi Li*

"Inquiry is about expanding your horizons and taking on challenges. For me, the experience has fostered personal development and an appreciation for life-long learning."
- *Natasha Nazarali*

"Inquiry is the foundation for self directing learning."
- *Hanieh Rahimi*

"Inquiry is the process of obtaining knowledge and skill relevant to one's own learning objectives. It is through this process that I have been able to identify my knowledge gaps and reflect upon my personal and academic growth."
- *Jillian Roberts*

'For me, Inquiry is about two things: Student Engagement and Student Empowerment. Either way it is a learning method that centres around the student."
- *Jonathan Sachs*

"Inquiry is a style of learning that can frustrate students to no end during the process, but leaves them with the most valuable lessons in the end. Thus, patience and perseverance are required in order to truly see its benefits."
-*Andrew Schepmyer*

"Inquiry is about taking the initiative to seek and discover the world around us and the world within us."
- *Michael Wang*

"Inquiry is an approach to learning that focuses on the learner. My Inquiry experiences have facilitated me to become accustomed to identifying purposes, looking at further implications, recognizing assumptions, and enhancing my personal set of values."
- *Henry Wong*